Wystan and Chester
*A Personal Memoir of*
*W. H. Auden and Chester Kallman*

# Wystan and Chester

*A Personal Memoir of*
*W. H. Auden and Chester Kallman*
*by* **THEKLA CLARK**

Introduction by
James Fenton

*Columbia University Press*
*New York*

First published in Great Britain by Faber and Faber Limited
3 Queen Square London WC1N 3AU

First published in the United States in 1996 by
Columbia University Press
562 West 113th St., New York, NY 10025
All rights reserved

Library of Congress Cataloging-in-Publication Data

Clark, Thekla.
Wystan and Chester : a personal memoir of W. H. Auden and Chester
Kallman / by Thekla Clark ; introduction by James Fenton.
p.   cm.
ISBN 0-231-10760-9 (cloth).
1. Auden, W. H. (Wystan Hugh), 1907–1973—Friends and associates.
2. Kallman, Chester, 1921–   —Friends and associates.
3. Poets, English—20th century—Biography.
4. Poets, American—20th century—Biography.
5. Clark, Thekla—Friends and associates.
6. Ischia Island (Italy)—Biography.
I. Title.
PR6001.U4Z637    1996
811'.52—dc20
[B]
96-8842

For Lisa, Anne and Irving, John and Simon
and with grateful thanks to
Michael Mallon, Darryl Pinckney and Lorna Sage

# Contents

# Illustrations

# Introduction
*by* JAMES FENTON

Auden's reputation as a poet has not always stood as high as it does today. Various kinds of attack have ceased and it is a long time, for instance, since I have read such a double denigration as greeted Humphrey Carpenter's biography in *The Times*, a review entitled 'Butterflies from the Dungheap' – the dung-heap being Auden, or Auden's personal life, the butterflies being the poems that somehow emerged from all that filth.

Auden the man tended, in the years soon after his death, to be remembered for what he had become in the depression of his last days, rather than for what he had been. As for the poems, there lingered a common English view, pioneered by Philip Larkin and writers of his generation, that dated a decline from Auden's move to the States at the end of the thirties. Auden had one decade as a poet, and that was that. Implicit in this view was the suggestion that the decline of the poetry was a punishment for a sort of treachery.

I have often wondered with what emotion Auden would have read Larkin's review of 1960, in which the deeply indebted younger poet said that 'No one is going to justify [Auden's] place in literary history by *The Shield of Achilles*, any more than Swinburne's is justified by *Poems and Ballads: Third Series*.' Remarks like that are designed to seek out and demoralize their objects, and the author of this memoir tells us that Auden tried not to read such reviews, but could be deeply wounded by remarks relayed. Such a pained avoidance of criticism, however, represents a retreat from the heroic posture Auden assumed after being attacked in print by Randall Jarrell. 'Jarrell's in love with me,' Auden said.

Auden suffered latterly, and his reputation suffered for a while. But it has become clear during the two decades since his death that a new Auden is being pieced together by people who do not (like Jarrell and Larkin) have to fight their way out from under an influence. This new Auden is the result of new readings, new information, new scholarship – scholarship that has begun most promisingly but still has a way to go. We have the dramatic works, the libretti, the astonishing juvenilia. But who can imagine what Auden's prose will look like when published complete? Or how the poems will read in the various kinds of edition that will come to complement the *Collected*? Who is to say what the letters will be like, or how the next biography will read (or how some future *Times* reviewer will react)?

All biographies are to some degree pretentious, when we bear in mind how little we know of our close acquaintances, let alone of a figure met with only in documents. What was the real nature of the relationship between Auden and Kallman? How can we sum such a thing up, if our friends surprise us with their divorces, if what looked like happiness turns out to have been a brave front, or if what looked like mutual torture turns out to have contained a mechanism for mutual support? Did Kallman destroy Auden's life? Such a question can only begin to be posed by someone who is also prepared to ask: did Auden destroy Kallman? There were after all two points of view, two sets of human rights involved.

Many of the perceptions in Thekla Clark's account struck me as entirely fresh, even though I have known her for many years and have often talked about these memories. One is the thought that, however much Wystan and Chester clashed, Chester never tried to undermine Wystan's work. Another is that, by the end, Chester was to Wystan like an impossible child, a thought which suggests its parallel, that Wystan was to Chester like an impossible parent, that *this* was the destructive force that he had to avoid. Thirdly there is the feeling that Wystan began to find life hard to face when he realized the extent to which Chester was falling apart, with its implication that Wystan's reliance on Chester had been much greater than even their close friends realized.

That Wystan was prepared to defer to Chester and to take a rebuke to heart – that I can bear witness to, as I was responsible for provoking an incident mentioned in this memoir. I was describing, after dinner in Kirchstetten, an experiment on the nervous system of an earthworm (I was studying neurophysiology) in which I had inadvertently sent a massive electric shock through the said worm, thereby killing it. Wystan hated this story, and exploded – not against me exactly, but against those who performed that kind of experiment. And of course I felt abashed to have told a story that produced such an effect. Chester's rebuke to Wystan was really a way of coming to my defence, without defending vivisection.

The conversation changed course. The windows and doors were, as ever, tight shut, and the smoke was terrific. Whether I was a bit teary, or it was just the fug, I don't know, but after a while I left the table and went for a breather in the kitchen. Soon Chester joined me, and I knew that he sensed I would have been quite upset. So I tried without saying as much comically to communicate the idea that I wasn't upset, it was just the smoke. But I was grateful to Chester, nevertheless, for seeing that I *might* have been *quite* upset. If you are in awe of a man, you do not necessarily want him to turn all his guns against you.

For the rest, I received nothing but kindness and consideration from Wystan. The first time we met, I was due to study in Florence, and he insisted that I should look up John and Thekla Clark. They, in turn, reintroduced me to Wystan, on a couple of those family visits described in this book. And now

Thekla has reintroduced us to Wystan and Chester, both as they were in happier times, and as they came to be when things went wrong. It's another act of friendship, one of a long series involving Wystan and Chester, Thekla and John, and that great circle of theirs.

# PART I

# Ischia

For years I had longed to be on the other side of the Atlantic. When I walked down the gangplank of the *Conte Biancomano* on to the dock at Naples I felt as though I had been on a monumental binge and was cold sober at last, blissfully and safely far from Oklahoma. The unknown language reduced sound to a blur; only imperatives were identifiable. There were so many people and so much movement; the sun was the only reality. It was shining on everything, even the shadows. Italy certainly seemed where I was meant to be.

I was still wearing white cotton gloves and was overly aware of the attention I was causing, but somehow I knew that life and I would never be the same. That the Italians were obsessed by all things American was conspicuously evident in Naples in 1951. Any young woman was a challenge, a blonde American a challenge it would have been a disgrace not to accept. Did I realize that the admiration was more commercial than personal? No! Did it matter? Not at all.

I was to be met by a young American poet, Anthony Hecht, at whose suggestion I had come to Europe. Tony and I had played together as children – our mothers were friends – but hadn't seen each other since. Nudged by our mothers, we had exchanged letters (his had accused me of wanting to place Gothic embellishments on the sand castles we once built together) and it was decided that I would visit him on Ischia, the island in the Bay of Naples where he lived, and where his friends included W. H. Auden and Chester Kallman. Standing at the rail of the ship I searched for him among the crowd waiting on the dock. The only obviously non-Italian young man I could see was pale, plump, with fluttering hands and dressed entirely in white; my heart sank. At the end of the gangplank, while I was warding off offers of all kinds, I heard someone call my name and looked around to find not the pale, plump young man but a lean, bearded beauty. I felt I had won the lottery.

The voyage over had been a star turn for me at twenty-four and, if I say so myself, quite nifty. Ten days on a luxury liner and although the cabins were smaller than expected and the orchestra scraggly, the liner's main stairway was ideal for making a grand entrance. The captain was a disappointment (short and dumpy) but the first officer was a dream. My father had insisted that I go First Class – a social disadvantage. First Class passengers were mainly Italo-Americans (some with families) who had made it big in the States and were going home to be admired; one dry-as-dust Professor (American) whose wife and children went Second; a scattering of businessmen and a mixed bag of tourists with a hopeful Mrs Stone or two. I had to cross the barricades to meet those exotic creatures the Fulbright scholars. With my *Teach Yourself Italian* in hand I practised on my companions at the purser's table. How pleased they were that I was attempting to learn, and how charming they found my mistakes!

The romantic-looking poet fitted in so well with all the other wonders it never dawned on me that he might not be the perfect match for an overconfident Daisy with her New World exuberance and vulgarity. Tony took charge of my luggage, negotiating to have it kept for us while we visited the city, his cautious Italian so much easier to follow than the free-flowing language I had heard aboard. I had promised myself that I would learn to see the Neapolitans as they really were, not as the colourful, primitive creatures of the movies. All pretence at that dissolved almost at once, and I delighted in people so exotic, so diverse that we might well be classified as different species. Superficial to be sure, but I decided to worry about depth later.

To exchange my dollars we entered a seedy, low-lying building near the dock, and walked through an unlighted corridor where an alcove at the end served as an office. There was a table and two chairs. Neither of the two unshaven, youngish men got up or even nodded when we arrived. From the ceiling hung a naked lightbulb, quite necessary as there were no windows, but of an incredibly low voltage. Electricity in 1951 was still a luxury to be doled out frugally. The business, deadly serious, of exchange was done with a contraption that was a cross between an abacus and an adding machine. It was as exciting as anything from a Bogart film.

We then took a quick jaunt around the city with my bare shoulders causing a semi-scandal in the *bassifondi*; I couldn't understand the words the women screamed at me, but their intention was clear. My delight in the colourfulness of the *quartieri* turned first to amusement and then to embarrass-ment. My first lesson in the value of noise as 'counter magic'. Learning to separate volume from intent took me a long time.

Conversation was easy, at least for me, as I tend to babble and I'm a great one for the sharp intake of breath to denote enchantment. Tony, poor lamb, confined himself to practical information. I remember his description of the customary period of mourning on the island; he said I was not to be astonished at the number of women dressed in black. That should have told me something.

Then, over an indifferent lunch (even for Naples), he began to tell me about his friends on Ischia, all of whom knew and respected Auden. It was difficult to separate and place all those new names. I tried to imagine what they, the names, would look like. I didn't get a single one right, although I was close about a German painter who didn't count for much in the overall picture anyway. We ate at the Ristorante Pappagallo. It was named after what was then one of the most famous restaurants in Italy – Pappagallo of Bologna – a very Neapolitan gesture. It was also quite Neapolitan to call it a 'ristorante' at all, as in any other city it could not have passed the 'trattoria' class. The beaded curtain at the entrance, only a vaguely successful screen for the invading flies; the dim light inside; the strange fan-like object going round and round over the freshly made pasta on display: all added to the excitement. I think I gained some respect for my appetite, it was probably unexpected that I would wolf down the whole of the simple pasta dish, the lukewarm tongue and the delicious green sauce. But I am an eater and the green sauce was a first-time joy. I also did my share of putting away the wine. Knowing that poets are traditionally starving I offered to pay my share, only to be told that I would be allowed to do so in the future, but not today.

I would have preferred a horse and carriage but we took a taxi to the dock (the Molo Beverello), arriving just in time for the last, the five o'clock, boat for Ischia. There were only two sailings a day and had we missed this one we would have had to spend the night in Naples, a prospect that seemed to terrify my poet.

It was the end of June, the weather was perfect and the sea calm. We could sit outside and none of the passengers was sick. Crossing even this small expanse of water was considerably less pleasant in bad weather. Custom decreed that once seated the passengers left their seats only to disembark. When necessary they turned their heads aside and threw up on the floor, noisily and cheerfully. Among the regular passengers there was almost a competition: 'Aai, was I sick today!' inferred superiority over the less sensitive. Rivers of pasta asciutta flowed. The crew members would get busy with buckets of sand and extraordinary goodwill. The passengers not actively sick sucked on enormous lemons and groaned. How the Italians ever had a navy . . . This particular day, however, was glorious and even the braying of the radio was not offensive; I was fascinated by the RAI (the Italian state radio) version of the nightingale's song at each change of programme. We had a whole bench to ourselves. I spread out my arms and legs, admiring my shipboard tan against the Nile green of my scandal-making dress; Tony put his head in my lap and pretended to sleep; all that chattering and enthusiasm must have been exhausting. We stopped at Procida and I tried desperately to remember where I had heard that name – I did so want to pass as an intellectual – but neither of us could produce *I Vespri Siciliani* so I just looked silly.

We got to Forio in time to deposit me and my luggage at the house, or more properly, part of a house, that Tony had rented for me. It was discreetly near, or far, from his. He must have regretted the invitation to come to Ischia, engineered by our mothers and issued, I am certain, with no idea that it would be accepted.

We were scheduled to meet friends, intellectuals of course, at a newly opened restaurant, the first in Forio, although there were several on the opposite, the fashionable, side of the island. The new restaurant – here again the title was presumptuous – was owned by an American, the first blemish on this idyllic setting. After dinner we were to go to The Caffè to meet the others, including Auden and Kallman. Dinner consisted of pizza, wine and grapes. The pizza, which took ages to make, arrived blessedly full of garlic and was quite edible; the local wine (slightly sour, murky white) grew on one, and the grapes were heaven. The tables had been set outside on a terrace with steps leading down to the narrow strip of sand bordering the sea. The view was breathtaking; I intook several times while waiting for the pizza. The couple at dinner with us were mid-to-late thirties and terribly good-looking. She small, red-headed with a sharp, long face and a quick and, I soon realized, devastating tongue. Conversation was excellent – I didn't need to babble at all. She told a very funny joke in which the word 'fuck' figured prominently. I felt that I had arrived! Her husband was earnest and rather boring but so handsome with his white tennis sweater draped over his shoulders that it didn't really matter. It didn't really matter until I unwisely offered an enthusiastic appraisal of a new Sean O'Casey play and he said, 'Oh, I suppose the hero dies on the church steps again, doesn't he?' A look exchanged with his wife finished the conversation and me off. The hero did indeed die on the church steps.

Evening life in Forio was centred on The Caffè, where The Table was reserved for Wystan, Chester and their friends. The owner of The Caffè was the famous Maria, who rated a column in the national newspapers when she died many years later. Its official name was Caffè Internazionale, but I never heard it called anything but 'Maria's'. Maria was square, both in body and face, and her hair was shoe-polish black, cut short with a centre parting often showing white on either side – a friend came from Naples every few months to 'do the colour'. Her caffè was a large, windowless room with two doors, one leading to a side alley and a huge one opening on to the square where the tables were set. What, I wondered, was it like in winter? 'Dank,' said Chester. 'Cosy,' said Wystan. She served the local white wine in glass decanters. For her favourites there were glass reproductions of Victor Emmanuel and Queen Elena. There was also a supply of soft drinks, beer, coffee made on the stove – no espresso machine in those days – and, for the very brave, Italian brandy. When we arrived, late according to Wystan's schedule, he and Chester were already seated at The Table together with an American couple, the Weisses, who became my close friends, the German painter, known to all the local lads as *Eduardo caro*, and a Nordic wearing long, lank hair and long, lank shorts who turned out to be a Swedish painter, silent and untalented.

Conspicuous in what would now be called 'designer' clothes, I acknowledged the 'hellos' and found myself seated next to Wystan as the newest arrival. I wish I could say it was friendship at first sight, but it was not, though I certainly did not feel the hostility that I felt from the little redhead and her husband. Chester was the star of the evening. I especially remember a hilarious story in a strong Neapolitan accent about cooking dried cod. It was a relief after the social tension to laugh and laugh. He was a brilliant storyteller and Wystan roared with appreciation. When the subject was changed to something intellectual – a series of essays I hadn't read by an author I'd never heard of – I could almost feel the satisfaction oozing out of the redhead. As Wystan rose to leave – he was always the first, like royalty – he turned to me and said, 'Tea tomorrow?' and looked to Chester for approval. It was immediately forthcoming and the invitation was seconded with the spontaneity and grace that was so very 'Chesterish'.

Tea turned out to be coffee. Tony and I were right on the dot of four-thirty – a fixation of mine for which I apologized, only to learn that Wystan was even more rigorous about schedules. We were off to a good start. Their house, like all Forio houses with any pretensions, was surrounded by a high white-washed wall. The gate swung open on to a courtyard where the owners did their farm work. Later in the summer huge braids of small, round tomatoes would hang down, to be picked off bit by bit during the winter. The last of last year's braids was almost empty and the remaining tomatoes were shrivelled and brown; the garlic and onion braids were fairly full and obviously in use. We passed through the courtyard, climbed an outside stairway and reached what could be called the *piano nobile*. We had coffee on a good-sized terrace and I mostly noticed how relaxed it all was. The only thing I remember was Wystan's comment to Tony that he should wean himself away from Yeats. 'How can anyone say "I have watched an hour"? Poetry must be accurate.' 'Or,' said Wystan, ' "The intellect of man is forced to choose / Perfection of the life or of the work." Completely untrue, you know – perfection is possible in neither.'

Just then Wystan and Chester were terribly excited at the prospect of going to Venice for the world première of *The*

*Rake's Progress*. Their admiration and affection for Stravinsky was immense. Wystan said that being asked to work with Stravinsky was the greatest honour he had ever received. Chester said what a pet Vera Stravinsky was!

The summer was bliss – for the most part anyway. At one point the redhead took me aside to say, 'I was so pleased when Tony called you "darling", I wanted to cheer.' Tony and I declared serious intentions in tones that neither of us believed, and we both knew that our farewell at the dock when I sailed back to America was just that – a farewell. What did last was the friendship with Wystan and Chester. It was to grow and grow, based mostly on shared laughter but also on the ease we found in each others' company. It certainly wasn't ever – with either of them – a relationship (horrid word) in which one went for ages without talking. None of those deep understanding silences so prominent in descriptions of friend-ship. Not at all, it was talk, talk, talk day and night. Any subject, nothing was too much or too little. They saw me through an unfortunate marriage to a handsome Italian, a dreary affair with an American academic, and rejoiced when I finally found my husband, John. 'I needn't tell you, need I,' said Wystan. 'We'd almost given up,' said Chester. 'Every loving wish for your loving happiness' said the telegram for our wedding, to which they couldn't come.

In 1952 I came back to Ischia for a four-month stay. This time I brought my daughter Lisa with me. Ischia was paradise for small children but the most important thing was that Wystan and Chester 'adopted' her even more quickly than they had 'adopted' me. She was almost two and until I married John, when she was ten, they were the fathers. Lisa never knew her biological father, who was killed by a hit-and-run driver in Los Angeles where she had been born. The son of unsuccessful opera singers, the father Italian, the mother English, he was a songwriter (born with perfect pitch) and a minimally successful actor, fourteen years older than I. Lisa inherited his beauty, though, unfortunately, not his musical gifts.

Lisa was her own person at two and Chester and Wystan both adored her. Wystan always claimed to be a little afraid of her; he felt she was taking notes even before she could write. Chester naughtily encouraged her in her little princess behaviour and was delighted when she insisted upon being 'given the *Lei*' (the formal address) when she was four. Chester wrote some enchanting poetry for her but, as it was out of character, it was never published. A pity because it avoided the archness so often found in verses for children. Chester conspired with her; Wystan spoke to her as though she understood.

I remembered one night in Ischia when I had guests and Lisa, aged four, kept coming into the room in her nightie. At her third appearance Wystan said, 'My dear, you are not wanted now.' It worked! The next day, as a reward, Wystan took out his teeth for her; she felt truly compensated. Wystan supervised her reading and was pleased when she loathed *Winnie the Pooh* without any prompting from him. He sometimes read to her himself; Beatrix Potter was a favourite when she was little, although I remember a dreadful row when each wanted to be Mrs Tiggywinkle in an elaborate game they played. Chester was called in to arbitrate and declared that Wystan, with his feet, could only be Jemima Puddleduck. Wystan began her collection of Andrew Lang fairy tales and was pleased when she burst into tears at the mere mention of 'The Yellow Dwarf' or 'The Wonderful Sheep'. I once came upon them after a reading to find Lisa in floods and Wystan saying it was quite right to weep as the tale was based on ritual and myth and as such needed to be believed. Lisa agreed to believe it only if Wystan would take his teeth out again.

One summer Wystan spent a great deal of time taking photographs; he did it very well. Two of the best photographs I have of Lisa as a small child were taken by him. 'Rather Alice, I thought,' he said.

Wystan as a photographer seemed out of character. What

was he after? I tried to find out, subtly (neither a talent of mine nor an effective approach to him). He offered no help – neither did he discourage my questions. The whole thing had turned into a game. Could I discover? Would he divulge? Wystan would never have bought an expensive camera and spent so much of his free time without a solid reason. He was deep into Malcolm de Chazal that summer; there was a great deal of talk about intelligent thumbs and youthful ears. Wystan loved the concrete, so I offered the 'fact' that Lisa (aged three) always requested a familiar story to be told to her at bedtime and then asked for it to be repeated. 'The lazy ear,' he said, 'to be expected.' 'Is the eager eye the answer then?' I asked. 'The answer to what?' he muttered infuriatingly. The camera disappeared the following summer. I took a perverse pleasure when I read, years later, a poem describing the diesel engine as 'a vile invention, more vicious, more criminal than the camera even'.

As Lisa grew older naturally her relationship with Wystan changed; fairy tales gave way to more sophisticated literature and to the abiding passion each had for grammar books and dictionaries. She introduced Wystan to the Beatles in exchange for Rilke.

The four-month stay in the summer of 1952 was so successful that Lisa and I repeated it every year until 1957. Ischia was (for me) the right size island; not as big as Elba where there was little feeling of being on an island; not as small as Capri which, for all its beauty, gave me claustrophobia. Each island town had a distinct character, as well as its own form of dialect. Porto was a popular Neapolitan resort and even in those days had a couple of respectable hotels; Casamicciola still showed signs of the earthquake it had suffered years ago before it had been host to Ibsen; Lacco Ameno had the best hot springs and was soon to have the island's first luxury hotel; Sant'Angelo was the most remote (there was no road, people and supplies arrived by boat, on foot or on donkey) and picturesque, soon to be taken over by Germans, while Forio was, and remained for a long time, the most 'Ischian' of all the towns. The centre of the island sported an extinct volcano, Epomeo, which Wystan kept saying he should climb but, as far as I know, never did. Chester never even pretended.

That summer of 1952 I rented what passed for a *signorile* house in town, overlooking the port. One of Mussolini's daughters had stayed there and the landlady, a devout Fascist, felt I was a comedown. An old law demanded that after three days a visitor register with the police. This was done automatically by hotels and pensions and was required from anyone who took in PGs. The law was a blessing to my *padrona di casa*. She brought out a double-entry ledger for me to sign and turned reverently to a frayed page with 'Edda Ciano' written in huge letters. The rent was 25,000 lire a month, a little more than forty dollars by the day's exchange. The ceilings of her house were high, the walls bone white, the terrace huge, but I never liked it.

The ideal beach, San Francesco, was about two kilometres out of town and we acquired a *carrozza* and driver. We didn't actually acquire them, but after the first day the carriage appeared, with Peppino the driver, in front of our door twice a day. Peppino was short and dark with uncombed black curls, a Mediterranean Harpo Marx. We were presented to his family of Mamma and nine siblings. Whenever I asked about Papa the Forians shook their heads and looked skyward. I understood when I saw a plaque on his carriage which said *Giuseppe Pino, n.n.* Years ago people were identified by paternity: Giovanni di Paolo (John son of Paul) or Giovanni fu Paolo if the father was dead. The Latin words for *n.n.* (*non noto*) mean unknown father. This formula was sometimes used by the rich and aristocratic to settle problems of inheritance. In this case it meant just what it said. My family sent packages from the US which helped feed and clothe the family, whose only asset was Peppino's horse and carriage. Girl Scout uniforms that had belonged to my sister were transformed by a tightening of a belt and unbuttoning of top buttons into very smart frocks. My father's old dinner jacket got one brother a job as a waiter in Porto, and an older sister left for Naples on the strength of my mother's silver lamé skirt.

The following summer we moved to a peasant house near San Francesco, where we stayed every summer for the next four years; during our last summer, in 1957, my parents were with us, so we needed a larger, more civilized house.

Our house in Via Cesotta had only three inside rooms and a bathroom of sorts. We spent most of our time in a room which was actually an extended pergola. The owners had laid down a cement floor; a line of bamboo on which morning glories climbed formed a wall (the flowers creating a constantly changing wallpaper) which separated the space from the surrounding tomato and zucchini plants; vines were the roof. Set in a vineyard, the house was reached by swinging open a green wooden door in the outside wall and then coming down a steep flight of steps, edged with discarded powdered milk tins, painted green and filled with geraniums. Here in this outside-inside room everything happened, meals, chats, children's games, parties, romances, passionate discussions. The property was owned by a family named Castaldi, whose matriarch was a weather-beaten dignified woman named Beatrice, with feet like a prophet's. There was a husband, but he counted for little (the property had come down through Beatrice's family). An older daughter had married into the middle class (her husband had a hardware store in Forio and she wore a hat to Mass instead of a scarf), a son was in the navy and a younger daughter, Restituta, worked for me. Saint Restituta is not in the *Penguin Dictionary of Saints* but she was very real on Ischia. It seems she arrived on the island, at Forio, during the reign of the Roman Emperor Valerian. She had been tortured in an effort to make her renounce her faith which naturally she refused to do. Placed in a burning boat at the mainland, she died praying and the boat sailed on to Forio with her remains. Whether the remains then came back to life was still a matter of discussion in Forio. She is portrayed with

14

a cross in one hand and a book in the other, which pleased Wystan, who referred to her as 'dear S.R.' Her intervention was sought for sexual or intellectual problems.

Tituta, as she was called, was still in her teens when we first arrived. She had a flat smiling face that was strangely attractive. That first summer her childhood love, Vito, whose family owned the adjoining vineyard, was being shipped out to a married sister in Australia. Tituta would never have been allowed to marry him since there was not enough land to go around and he had three older brothers. During those weeks before he sailed, they could be found squatting on the dirt road which separated his house from ours, close together, often weeping, but never, so far as I could see, touching. He was sent away, and Tituta recovered although she did not marry until years later.

For Lisa and me Tituta was everything: companion, nurse, maid, Italian teacher, pasta maker, and the running water I had been promised when I rented the house. The water ran when Tituta, barrel on her head, climbed a ladder and poured it into the cistern on the roof. One summer she even saved Lisa's soul: she had her secretly baptized while I was in Naples. 'Don Gaetano smiled at me,' said Lisa on my return. 'That's nice, dear,' I replied. 'Yes, he smiled when he put the water on my head, and smiled and smiled.' Wystan was incensed as he had very definite ideas concerning the limitations of any priest's role – 'a rather superior butler' he said. I, however, was going through a Graham Greene phase and was intrigued. It was the first time I openly defied Wystan on an important matter. He said I should complain, even write to the Bishop and have Don Gaetano reprimanded. One night in his cups he went so far as to say defrocked. The matter was considered too trivial to raise much interest at The Caffè; a fact that drew Wystan and me together. We knew how important it really was.

Lisa and I were the envy of the zone, what with our running water, the electricity that worked most of the time, and our wooden icebox which was kept supplied with blocks of ice brought every other day on the head of a neighbour. Carrying loads on their heads was a talent of the islanders; baskets full of grapes or tomatoes were a common sight, but even the Forians stopped to praise the hawker I once saw with a stack of white dinner plates piled high on his head.

The sea was about two hundred yards from our house. The deep sandy beach was really a cove bounded on one side by a dramatic rocky promontory (the luxury villas of today were not yet built), and on the other by a grassy plateau with a single whitewashed house. The beach was empty until the Feast of San Giovanni, the 24th of June, because the Forians considered it dangerous to bathe before then. On San Giovanni local families came to the beach to pay their respects to the sea. The older men took off their shirts, the younger ones rolled up their trousers, the children put on bathing suits and went in the water up to the waist, the women of all ages busied themselves with the food. They came back on August 15th, the Feast of the Assumption, but not in between.

Lisa had friends as there were two and later three American families with children near her age. Wystan came out often in the late afternoon with his dog, Mosè. Chester didn't care for the beach, his smooth tan was acquired sunbathing on the terrace, and Wystan came for the walk and the tea afterwards. We met most mornings in town before or after the shopping and nearly every night either for dinner or afterwards at Maria's. Our routines fitted nicely as the muse and a young child are equally demanding and at more or less the same hours. The daily shopping also imposed a certain schedule. Ischia's only export was wine, so arable land was devoted to vines and, apart from vegetables from small family patches and a few (very few) chickens and rabbits, everything had to come from the mainland. The lack of proper refrigeration conditioned the size of the shopping, and the miserable quality of the meat the menu. Wystan and Chester were always at Maria's for coffee around eleven, having already put in four or five hours' work. We met there to receive the day's mail which came on the morning boat, compare shopping lists and make plans for the evening. Only on rare occasions did we lunch together.

Life was so pleasant that I seldom left the island – a shopping trip or the opera in Naples, which meant at the most one night away, and then a hurried return. I did, however, take a sightseeing trip to Rome and Florence, where I acquired the handsome Florentine lover whom I made the mistake of marrying later.

A wonderful American couple, Anne and Irving Weiss, lived near us. Their first child, a daughter Lisa's age, had been born on the island, the first American as far as anyone knew. One of the few cars available had been ordered weeks in advance to take Anne to the hospital in Porto. Calling the Maternità a hospital was like calling the Pappagallo a 'ristorante'. It was a large square house built probably as a seaside villa early in the century. There was a luxuriant garden, a delivery room and nuns' quarters downstairs. Upstairs there were seven beds and an office. There was a doctor but Anne saw him only briefly; she was delivered by the local *ostetrica* (midwife). The catering was extraordinary. A nun would come in the morning and announce which vegetables in the Maternità's garden were ready to be picked and Anne made her choice. She often heard her supper squawk as its neck was being wrung. She asked to be excused from 'drinking' a freshly laid egg (an Italian custom). A nun would come in every morning, sit by her bed, gossiping and beating up the yolk of a raw egg and sugar until it was a frothy cupful. Anne says she went on to have three more children because of her blissful stay in the Maternità.

Among the foreigners there were at that time two distinct societies (the fashionable crowd came later). There was the family/intellectual set, to which Lisa and I belonged, as did Wystan and Chester; we were a serious lot, as proven by caffè conversations and exchanges of books and articles. Then there was what would today be called the 'gay' set. This group varied enormously: a member of a royal family, a floating group of designers, painters and just plain 'lovelies'. Wystan and Chester didn't belong to this group (I was an honorary member because of my extensive wardrobe, pieces of which I willingly loaned for special occasions); they disapproved of some of its members and avoided the continual round of parties. Wystan stayed away because he found most of the group uninteresting. Chester's motives were more complex. He objected to what he called the 'faggot-chic'. One year they sublet their house for the winter to a painter/designer and came back to find it with new black curtains, cushions and candles everywhere. Chester was furious. He also thought it wrong that the group's local boyfriends were strictly for hire and never seen or mentioned in any other context. When Wystan's brother John, his wife and daughters came to stay, we all went to Alessandro's (Chester's local boyfriend) for a family meal.

Forio was incredibly poor. A story of Chester's always makes me laugh, but it is a tender laugh. When he first arrived in Ischia, alone, he was taken by a local boy into the family vineyard. Once there the boy made it abundantly clear that for 500 lire (less than a dollar even then) Chester could have him and all the grapes he could eat.

Although it didn't meet all his requirements, Wystan agreed that Forio qualified as a moderate Eden. Eden was temporary and ours was no exception. Forio was for me a testing ground. I was establishing the boundaries, the limitations beyond which I couldn't go. Perhaps it was my age; but I think it was more the place, the company, the suspended quality of life. During the fifties life on Ischia was, for me, indeed blessed; free from anxiety and full of outward joy. Under that fierce southern sun the colours were clearer, the dividing lines sharper than I had ever experienced. It was wonderfully good for me, for us all. Wystan and I talked about it, saying it couldn't, shouldn't, last. Chester said he refused even to think about it ending. In a strange way everything was what it appeared to be. Ischia is known locally as the *isola verde*, the green island, but when I see it in memory I see it as blue and white, the white of the houses and the blue of the sea and the sky. When I think of it I think of Wystan striding along with that dreadful dog of his, swinging a soiled string bag crammed with books and the day's shopping. When I asked him years later if he really had been the person he appeared to be – that enchanted foreigner trying to belong – he said, 'Yes, and that is why I had to leave.'

As Americans, some of us had come to Europe looking for what we didn't have – history. On Ischia we found not only history but myth as well. With the Ancient Greeks and Romans the more fortunate a person was the more godlike he appeared. Here we were, rich beyond belief (by island standards), blond, young, handsome, conquerors, and happy. The gods in those ancient myths were, after all, the same as humans, only their power was different. I asked Wystan if accepting adoration was bad for my character. 'Of course,' he said, 'but enjoy it.' All the worship was invigorating but it left me open to scorn when I mentioned it one night at The Caffè. 'Certainly all the locals want to sleep with you,' said the redhead. 'They've only had American *men* so far.' I hadn't mentioned sex or thought about it. If there was resentment about the foreign invasion of Forio, it was artfully concealed. I so fancied my new status as goddess that I listened without interest to the speculation at The Caffè. What did it matter? We were, or should have been, delighted, and the islanders either enjoyed adoring or could take pleasure in the fact that they had fooled the conquering foreigners. We played the parts assigned to us, our unpronounceable names changed by the Forians into indicators like *lo scrittore*, the writer; *lo studioso*, the scholar; I was *la biondona*, the big blonde. The important thing was to play the parts well. It was as though we lived in the third person; we were what we appeared to be to others. Wystan studied it, I revelled in it and Chester accepted it unquestioningly.

Early on Wystan involved me in a dilemma – not exactly a moral one – that created hours of discussion at The Caffè. There was a member of the 'gay' set in Forio, an ageing American whom I found singularly unpleasant. He was sullen when sober and fawning when drunk, obnoxious in either condition. He decided to marry the sister of his local boyfriend and asked Wystan to be his *testimone* at the wedding. Since the brother/boyfriend, who had the lovely name of Giocondo, worked for Wystan and Chester and they were fond of Franca, Wystan accepted. There was to be a church ceremony with the bride's numerous family and a select group of foreigners. Printed invitations were sent out, an exciting novelty for Forio, and a nuptial feast was planned. How, wondered members of the intellectual set, could Wystan take part in such a ceremony, knowing what he did about the groom's past and more than likely future? Wystan felt no need to justify himself to the others, but when he asked me to accompany him to the ceremony he offered an explanation, although I hadn't asked for one. 'Do come and sit with me,' he said, 'and wear a dark dress. It will be uncomfortable, but repentance is like forgiveness, unpredictable, and should be given a chance, no matter how slight.' The local church was packed and the priest in his sermon praised the good brother who introduced his dear friend to his beloved sister. Chester refused to attend, also missing was the bride's mother! Chester refused because he loathed the bridegroom; the bride's mother because she didn't hold with sex even if it was sanctified.

Thinking back, I suppose the first inkling of trouble came as early as 1951, although I certainly wasn't fully aware of it at the time. Wystan and Chester were preparing to go to Venice for the world première of *The Rake's Progress*, and Chester suggested that he might take Alessandro with him. Alessandro, whose last name meant 'tiller of the soil', was a peasant boy who had been Chester's lover for the last two summers. He was a quiet lad who did most of his talking through Chester, of whom he seemed genuinely fond. I remember my noble Italian lover was appalled when Alessandro 'gave me the *tu*' (the familiar address); things were different in those days. When Wystan told Chester that it was absurd to bring Alessandro, Chester answered, 'Well, you're bringing *me*.' Chester told the story himself at The Caffè one night, and although it was greeted with laughter – as no doubt Chester had intended it to be – I was uncomfortable.

Chester enjoyed flouting the social customs of the island, and inviting Alessandro to The Table was one way of doing so. At Maria's, the tables in the evening were taken by foreigners or by local men whose positions were firmly established (the town notary or a retired ship's captain); no women ever, except foreigners. A counterpoint to The Caffè life was the Forians' evening stroll, known as the *passeggiata*, which began as the sun was setting and continued until first the girls and boys, and then the pyjama-coated men were summoned home. The prescribed walk was from the main piazza where the buses stopped, up the hill to the church of Santa Maria del Soccorso overlooking the sea, and back. Maria's was almost in the middle. After the first few nights I was no longer aware of the people in the street; they had become a movement, a sound, a part of the surroundings. I mentioned this to Wystan who said, 'Of course' (a conversational tic not, he assured me, intended to belittle another's ideas) 'a view from a distance – actual or imagined – reduces history to nature', and left me with that. The young girls who made the *passeggiata* always walked on the side of the street opposite The Caffè, to avoid contagion. Our morals, as understood by the Forians, were acceptable for 'gods' and foreigners but were not to be acknowledged or endorsed openly. Chester bringing Alessandro to The Table was an open rebellion; having dinner at Alessandro's house was not. None of Wystan's lovers ever came to The Table, nor were they ever mentioned. The only exception was one whom he had set up in a barber shop. 'Cost less than dinner at the Ritz,' said Wystan, who was pleased at the shop's success. The shop long outlasted the romance.

Wystan was disappointed that, in spite of hints suggesting his availability, he had never been asked to march in local religious processions. There was a part of him that longed for a conventional life. It was what made him pay bills upon receipt, answer letters by return and pretend that the house was in order. He wasn't concerned with appearances, it was 'mother' that he answered to, 'mother' being that well-ordered family life that he remembered and used as a standard.

In the fifties Ischia was discovered by a great many famous or near-famous people, most of whom called on Wystan upon arrival. This was amusing for us but made no impression on the Forians. The arrival of an American film crew created far more excitement. Vast sums of money were dispensed, and the glamour was almost overwhelming. A full-rigged pirate ship was anchored at Porto, gigantic, long-haired Vikings swaggered through the streets; it was a week to remember. One night we were seated at a caffè in Porto, at a festa in honour of the local patrons, Saints Peter and Paul, listening to the band play an overture from, of all things, *The Red Poppy*. At a certain moment the noise changed key (one couldn't say a hush fell over the crowd, as nothing could 'hush' an island crowd) and Burt Lancaster surrounded by some definite Hollywood types came on to the terrace of The Caffè. He walked straight over to Wystan and introduced himself, saying how much he admired Wystan's work. That gesture meant far more to the islanders than a hundred Arthur Koestlers. And, after Chester and I had explained to Wystan who Burt Lancaster was, he, too, was pleased. Usually public recognition embarrassed Wystan. He admitted it gave him a certain satisfaction, but he often handled it badly. Once a young painter, upon being introduced to him at my house in Forio, said, 'Not *the* W. H. Auden?', and Wystan answered 'Is there another?'

Ischia in the fifties was so remote from anything I had ever experienced that life there assumed a theatrical quality. I sometimes felt that I was watching us all (including myself) perform. The physical setting, the enclosure of island living, even the weather (it was always beautiful, it never rained) all added to the effect. The rest of the world seemed dark and unsunned and uninteresting. This was the first and only time in my life that I can remember that everything was 'getting better'. There was peace. The grinding poverty of the islanders was slowly diminishing. I remember the excitement of the first wrapping paper at a food shop – no more old newspapers. At the same time, poverty was not yet considered shameful and the islanders managed to get comfort and pleasure from what seemed to us very little. A favourite treat was *pane-pommodoro*. This was made by taking the end of a pointed loaf, scooping out the centre, squeezing in tomatoes, mixed with salt, pepper and oil, and then replacing the inside of the bread. A delicious mess, and one Lisa and I soon came to love, although we didn't rely on it for a full meal as some Forians did. Cigarettes and eggs could be purchased singly, and pasta was weighed out by the *etto* (100 grammes) and kept in large glass-fronted wooden drawers. Maria installed a toilet one year, promising one that flushed for the near future. The first year when I asked to use the loo she produced a white enamel basin from behind the bar, and couldn't understand my reluctance to use it. The new vulgarity hadn't had time to set in seriously. I felt that Forio was a place that had yet to disappoint or be disappointed. That would certainly come, but I hoped it would come later, much later. To my mind we and the islanders had entered upon the adventure in good faith. There were arguments at The Caffè; I was accused of being romantic and naive, which I undoubtedly was. 'Can't you see that when those children you find so charming call to you for *cioccolate* they are really hurling insults?' I was asked. I couldn't, I wouldn't, I didn't see. Chester took my part in these discussions but Wystan never weighed in either for or against. We soon developed a routine, the children and I. Clever as they were, they learned that cries of 'cioccolate' yielded far less than smiles and compliments. If the balance was never perfectly struck, I preferred to err on the side of innocence – mine. I suppose that today it would be called a clash of cultures, but it seems to me that both we foreigners and the islanders tried our best to smooth things out. I often made mistakes.

One summer I brought with me from America a set of diaphragms at the special request of the tailor's wife. She was a lovely twenty-four-year old who already had three children. Since it was not only personal, but illegal as well, I wanted to keep it a secret, but that proved impossible. I was teased at The Caffè and compared to the eccentric Englishwoman who spent a small fortune buying hats for carriage horses in Naples and Rome. Wystan came to my rescue, saying surely there was a difference between horses' heads and women's cunts. I was saved but abashed.

Ischia had been a holiday spot for centuries. Ancient Romans came here to bathe in the hot springs for which the island was famous. The tradition continued, although the accommodation had become far from grand, almost primitive, in fact.

There were baths all over the island, even one very simple one in Forio. The idea of taking 'a cure' wasn't congenial, but the baths were. Lisa and I went regularly and I even used them to do laundry, washing out underwear that wouldn't stand up to Tituta's serious scrubbing. We were among the honoured clients, but everyone was welcome; Wystan even brought Mosè and there were no complaints, except from the dog himself. Mosè, as the name implies, was a foundling, whose character had not been ennobled by suffering. Wystan and Chester found him badly battered and took him in as a pup. Giocondo, whose job as houseboy included looking after Mosè during the winter, took very good care of him, trying to groom him to appear less of a mutt. I am a dog lover, have always had dogs, and like most dogs I know. Not this one, and it wasn't just what he did to my father later either. Chester made excuses for his behaviour but Wystan worried. Both Wystan and Chester were devoted to their pets but to Chester they remained 'pets'.

Wystan developed a strong attachment to one of our dogs; a black and white shaggy mongrel. They would have long conversations, each imitating the other. John Pope-Hennessy, a friend of ours, claimed that dogs made him feel emotionally inadequate. 'They are always so happy to see one,' he said, 'and one is only mildly happy to see them.' With Wystan it was quite the opposite. That animals possessed souls was one of his favourite arguments with my John, who was far more orthodox. Wystan spoke to Jackie in the same tones he used when speaking on the telephone. I suggested to Chester that we tape the collected telephone and canine conversations of the poet. 'And then John Cage could set them,' he said.

Once when I was staying with Wystan in Ischia – it was his fiftieth birthday, February 1957, and Chester was in the States – I came in late from a friend's house and he rushed to greet me on my return, naked. 'Oops,' said a disappointed Wystan. 'Sorry,' said I, and we both hurried off to our respective beds. The next morning we laughed about it, but neither of us ever mentioned it again.

I had arrived from Florence bearing the leg of lamb (actually two legs, as Italian lambs are small) that Wystan had requested for his birthday treat. A small dinner party was held at his friend Neil Little's villa, followed by a larger party for Forians and a few foreigners. Wystan was pleased with the number of telegrams that had arrived with birthday greetings. Telegrams were an event then in Forio. They were written out by hand and delivered by a little old lady on a bicycle, in due time. Wystan was especially pleased by a message from Moscow (in those days a faraway place) signed 'Gay Burgess'. Long before its present usage we found the 'Gay' very funny, although we will never learn if it was intended to be so.

That winter, 1957, was a difficult time for Wystan. He had tried staying in Ischia all year round, without Chester. He came to Florence twice and made as many other trips as possible, but he was still terribly lonely. He was also bound up in his theories about male menopause. He was cross with me because I couldn't enlighten him about hot flashes. And I, being thirty, was cross with him for asking. It was the only time I heard him express any doubts about his work, not a single piece, but the whole thing. 'I'm a clown,' he said, and when I answered, 'A sacred one' (I couldn't think of anything else to say), he said, 'No, but a transatlantic one at least.' We went for long walks and both agreed that it was loneliness, a rainy winter and, that wonderful excuse, male menopause. On one of our walks Wystan said to me, 'You women are so fortunate, you know why you're here. I'm adrift.' I tried to be a comforter, and suggested that these moments were only temporary. 'You Americans,' he said, 'to you time implies hope.' The conversation was going nowhere; I had no answer and Wystan had no intention of continuing. We walked along in a rare silence until we came to a bend in the road. There was 'Harvard' (Wystan's name for the village idiot) leaning on a rock, looking out to sea and masturbating. We went home and had a drink, twenty minutes ahead of schedule.

On one of his visits to Florence that year, when Alberto, my Florentine lover, and I were living in Piazza Bellosguardo, Wystan took me to lunch with the Sitwells, Edith and Osbert, at the family villa, Montegufoni, near Florence. The day before, we had lunched in great style and discomfort with Guido Chigi (great patron and founder of the Chigiana Music Academy) at his palace in Siena. The service plates were gold, the waiters' jackets so starched one wondered how they moved, the food pretentious. The conversation was stilted and dull when it wasn't downright offensive. Living in the palace was Ezra Pound's companion, the violinist Olga Rudge. She had wanted to meet Wystan, who had been one of the judges who awarded Pound the Bollingen Prize in 1949 and had defended his poetry. That did not mean that he supported, or even excused, Pound's political ideas. Wystan behaved with frigid politeness throughout lunch. I, as the youngest and most unimportant guest, kept quiet and smiled a lot. That is, I kept quiet until our hosts began attacking America's treatment of the great man. Words like malevolent, criminal and degenerate flew about. 'Well,' I said, 'the British hanged Lord Haw-Haw.' I was rewarded by an emphatic 'Indeed' from Wystan and a smile from our fellow guest, Luigino Franchetti (himself a musician and half Jewish). We did not stay for coffee. Years later I was 'cut dead' by Miss Rudge when we met at the festival at Spoleto; I was flattered that she remembered.

I apologized to Wystan for taking him there, and congratulated him on his forbearance. 'This will be different,' he assured me on our way to Montegufoni. How right he was! First of all the Sitwell house in Montegufoni was heated, overheated perhaps, but blissful after the draughts of the grand palace in Siena. The service was simple country and the food superb. Best of all, naturally, was the conversation. We talked about everything: from Philip Larkin's poetry, which Dame Edith didn't like – those bicycle clips – to midgets, to adventuresses (a favourite topic), to theology, all larded with just plain gossip. 'Verses to sex to God, quite proper,' said Wystan on the way home. Dame Edith was dressed in a long black skirt, black blouse and cardigan and wore a regally placed black pillbox hat. She was armed (I can think of no better word) with a huge black handbag, which she took into lunch with her. She was wonderfully nice to me, even took off her dark (black) glasses to look me over. We toured the house and since Osbert was suffering from Parkinson's disease and Dame Edith was too grand, we were taken around by Osbert's friend David Horner. He was tall, well dressed and looked far younger than his age, whatever that might have been. He was known, Wystan told me afterwards, as 'a rose-red sissy, half as old as time'. I understood the venomous look Dame Edith threw at his back as we left on our tour, where he kept saying things to us like *our* Severini'. The thing that made the deepest impression on Wystan was old Sir George's library, which had been bought by the yard. The volumes on the top shelves were bound in black leather and contained titles like *The History of the World War* in six volumes with no author's name, and *The History of India* in five volumes possibly by the same hand. The lower rows were filled with red leather volumes slightly smaller in size. They had left it as it was, explained Osbert, so that people could see what their father had been like. He and Edith kept *their* books in their own rooms. They treated Wystan and me as children home for the holidays, and seemed interested in everything we had to say, with Dame Edith nodding her head from time to time to indicate we had made considerable progress that term. Naturally, I was pleased and flattered but I was surprised to learn, on the drive home, that Wystan felt much the same way. Dame Edith's famous hands, covered with huge amethyst and topaz rings, made me think of a story that was going around Florence. It seems that Harold Acton's remarkable mother was heard to say, 'Tell me, Dame Edith, do you take off your beautiful rings when you type out your lovely poems?' (Some said it was actually 'lovely little poems' but I don't believe it. Mrs Acton was far too clever to overgild.) There are many other stories about Mrs Acton. The only time I saw her was when I had been in Florence a short time and was taken to the famous Acton villa, La Pietra, for drinks. She was then a handsome old lady, beautifully turned out, with an intelligent twinkle. She mixed the Martinis herself, with her acolyte, the butler, standing by to hand her the ingredients, and they were as powerful as any I have ever tasted. She led the conversation, and had a remark for every category of person present. Some of my fellow guests were academics, so university life and morals were quickly, and efficiently, dispatched. There was a French painter, an obvious homosexual, so that was easy. Then she turned to me. I was, for lack of anything more interesting, 'the young', so she said, 'The trouble with the young today is that they lack humility. Every morning I stand in front of my full-length mirror and say to myself, "Today you're going to be a bore to someone."' What a heavenly woman! I was so delighted that I sent this line to Wystan in a special delivery letter and he used it on a radio talk-show in New York the next week.

On one of Wystan's Florentine visits we went to pay our respects to Bernard Berenson at I Tatti. We were not a success. Cyril Connolly told me later how much Berenson disliked Wystan; as though I hadn't noticed. Also at tea were an American couple, the husband an aspiring painter with a handsome wife and a comfortable income. The wife and I were seated either side of our host and the interest he showed in us was unexpected and, I suppose, flattering. Wystan was soon in animated conversation, in German, with Nicky Mariano, Berenson's companion, which seemed to displease Berenson. It was a sticky forty minutes or so. The tour of the house was not an improvement either. The young woman who accompanied us stopped in front of each painting and told us, in considerable detail, just how Mr Berenson felt when he looked at it. Wystan declined to discuss the visit, except to say how perfect everything was and how he longed to slip a satin pillow with 'Souvenir of Atlantic City' into the place. I was reminded of one of Wystan's games: purgatorial pairs. The purpose was to define two people whose temperaments were so diametrically opposed that they would instantly loathe each other. This pair should then be bound together until each could understand, appreciate or even love the other. An example of Wystan's was T. S. Eliot and Walt Whitman, or even more extreme, Tolstoy and Oscar Wilde. I thought of Wystan and Berenson; and wondered how many centuries would pass before they came to appreciate one another.

*

Like Wystan, I was a well-loved child. It does, of course, make a difference in one's life, for which I was grateful, as was he. There was once a long and rather silly argument at The Caffè about the advantages of an unhappy childhood, especially for an artist. Wystan and I ranged against the others; we could see no advantage at all. A well-loved child finds it easier, as an adult, to love himself (to me the basis for all other love). He finds it easier to create a self that meets the requirements of the outside world, without denying his own personal needs. The memories of that circle of family affection stand him in good stead all his life. Once learned, the lesson that the giving of love can be a free and unconditional act is unforgettable. Once when I complained to Wystan about Lisa he said, 'Don't worry about her, she knows she is loved.' I asked Wystan if he had been his father's or his mother's favourite. 'Both,' he said. I laughed and Chester snorted. It wasn't the answer that was interesting but its strangely modest tone. Wystan's parents were 'good', loving parents which, I think, made him more tolerant towards Chester, the under-loved.

When Alberto, my Italian lover, first came to Ischia I worried that the mixture wouldn't work. He was no intellectual, so the caffè talk would not interest him; his English was sketchy so jokes would be difficult to follow, though he did enjoy a laugh. I need not have worried. He flattered the redhead, flirted with Chester and listened reverently to Wystan. He disapproved of Alessandro, on social not sexual grounds, but kept this from Chester. He was a great success. Only the redhead and Wystan dissented from the enthusiastic majority. She thought that Alberto, acceptable as a lover, would make a very bad husband. At the time I put her objections down to the comparison with her own (to my mind) pedestrian marriage; but she was right and I was wrong, even about her marriage, which turned out to be melodramatic and not at all pedestrian. Wystan's objections were more serious. He said he felt the presence of a mirror whenever he saw

Alberto. He was, of course, right. Alberto was forever search-
ing for his own image, which he loved to distraction not just
because it was beautiful, as indeed it was, but because it was
to him the most important thing in the world. Still more
serious was Wystan's objection to Alberto as a father for Lisa.
He asked me if I was certain that I wanted Alberto as 'a father
for my children'; I was far from certain, and Wystan and
Chester never accepted him as such.

One night at dinner at their house, Wystan said as Alberto
was hovering over me, 'You mustn't behave like newlyweds.'
This as he was stroking Lucina, the cat. Any outward show of
affection unnerved him. I remember years later he told me of
the dinner they gave T. S. Eliot and his wife in New York. The
Eliots were so involved in each other, so devoted, they asked
not to be separated by seating arrangements at the table.
When Wystan told me about the dinner party I think he
expected a laugh or at least a smile. I found the story moving
and said so. After all, if anyone had earned the happiness he
was then enjoying it was Eliot. 'Happiness, like grief, should
be private,' said Wystan.


With certain paintings the details must be absorbed before one
can make sense of the whole (I'm thinking of Constable but
I'm sure there are others). That last summer, 1957, that I spent
on Ischia, was like one of those paintings. It has taken over
thirty years for me to put all the bits and bobs together.
Important changes had already taken place offstage – my
mother's illness, Wystan's decision to leave Ischia. On the
island, outward evidence of change surrounded us. Signs of
growing prosperity and worsening taste: a row of oleanders
planted along the sea walk, flashy new additions to old
houses. Piles of sand, sacks of cement stood in front of
unsuspecting houses, able-bodied men were mixing cement
by hand, hammering, sawing, perched on ladders or down
holes, building, building, building. The promontory above
San Francesco sprouted a series of luxury villas with discreet

landscaping that would have been a welcome addition – anywhere else. A new set of gods had appeared. Alberto was more 'in demand' than Wystan and suddenly Chester had become 'disreputable'.

In February, when I was staying with Wystan for his birthday, I found that Peppino had abandoned his horse and carriage for a smelly new motorcycle-driven taxi. It wasn't too bad when open, but the fumes from the exhaust in the closed carriage were nauseating. I was happy for Peppino who delighted in the speed, the noise and his new clothes, but I longed for the comforting smell and the gentle plop of horse shit. Wystan and I often walked barefoot (victims of tormented feet), and the avoidance of manure piles was almost part of the pleasure. It was an improvement for the Forians that there were now three telephones in the town instead of the single one at the post office. I had once spent close to four hours there trying to get a call through to Rome. There was one at the doctor's house and one at the Bar Centrale. This bar, in the large square where the buses that circled the island stopped, and the *passeggiata* began, now considered itself Maria's rival. The telephone had been offered to Maria who, perhaps thinking of her foreign clientele, refused it. Happily, except for the addition of an espresso machine, Maria's hadn't changed.

She received with the dignity of a duchess in her caffè. I once saw a newspaper picture after a Royal Command Performance in which Joan Crawford 'received' Queen Elizabeth with a similar gesture. I can't remember seeing Maria away from The Caffè in all the years I went to Forio. Local gossip whispered about an unhappy romance in her youth, probably to explain her unmarried state, rare on the island, and unheard of for a woman in Maria's financial position. She was very attached to her widowed sister, Gisella, and her two sons. One nephew, Antonio, was known as a 'dish', and Chester called him Adonis. The other was known as a *topo di sagrestia* (church mouse). Antonio had the round eyes and the full lips of a putto, a rather soiled one. Salvatore looked 'wanting'. In contrast to her energetic and confident sister, Gisella was frail and sickly. She often sat quietly in the sun while one or the other of her sons combed her long black hair. They were equally gentle, and sometimes Antonio would sing to her softly.

As I was leaving Forio after my first summer I asked Maria what she wanted me to bring her from America the following year. She answered as though she had been expecting the question. She wanted an American dress; a daunting request, given her shape. A serious effort produced a discreet silk dress – small yellow flowers on a black background. When I gave it to Maria I received a gracious nod and a huge glass of Stock brandy; the dress was never seen again. At the end of the second year the request was repeated, with the same results. This went on each year, only from then on I put in my annual order using the Sears Roebuck catalogue. The mystery of the disappearing dresses was never solved. That last year I brought two dresses but asked to be excused from the brandy.

Chester and Alessandro were waiting at the dock when we (my parents and I) arrived for the last summer. For the first time I drove off the boat on a ramp instead of the usual two wobbly planks. The excitement was less, the assembled crowd thinner. 'Mercy!' said Chester as we embraced; a word he used for disapproval as well as wonder. Only later I learned that he meant my father's good looks. That year's house was 'grand', relatively speaking, although there was a room missing. When I contracted for it in April it was still being done up and there were definitely three bedrooms, plus a maid's room. Now in June there were two. The owner was a German named Fritz, Heinz or something similar, with an accent straight from Central Casting. He had emigrated to Argentina as soon as possible after the war – I was progressing from a Fascist landlord to a Nazi. Fortunately his English was non-existent, his Italian ludicrous, and I don't speak German.

His penny-pinching was a blessing as it kept him from indulging his taste around the house, and we made do by doubling up. A large open terrace overlooked the sea and there were geraniums planted among the volcanic rocks surrounding it.

Wystan and Chester took an immediate liking to my parents. My sophisticated mother understood the situation and was soon gossiping and laughing with them both. My father shook his head at certain of Chester's mannerisms; he hadn't come across anything like them in Oklahoma.

One night at dinner at their house, my father bent down to pat Mosè and was rewarded by a vicious bite in the fleshy part of his hand. He and Wystan and I went off to the local first-aid station while Chester and my mother repaired to Maria's. 'I shouldn't like to die here' was Wystan's comforting remark as we walked into the dimly lit, airless room. My father was much admired for his courage. Twelve stitches were administered with what looked like a cobbler's tool, the only anaesthetic a series of cigarettes supplied by Wystan. Wystan was impressed with my father because 'he didn't seem pleased with his own bravery'.

My mother had been operated on earlier in the year for cancer. The operation was relatively simple and had gone well. My father and I knew that the lymph glands had been affected and the prognosis was dismal, but we kept this from her. I told this to Wystan who said firmly, 'She knows, too.' One afternoon my mother, Wystan and I were drinking tea on our terrace, the first and only time we three were alone together. I felt that they had something to say to each other. I said I was going for a walk, and asked Wystan if he wanted to join me. He didn't. I walked through the vineyards and across the road towards the mountain, instead of the usual sea road. When I came back my mother was by herself, lonely but serene. We never spoke of that afternoon, although I kept hoping she would bring it up. When my mother died, a year later, she died in a state of grace. Going through her papers after her death I found a note from Wystan, from his St Mark's Place apartment in New York, in which he told her how much he had enjoyed seeing her that summer and that he was certain she 'would do it properly'.

That last summer was full of departures, actual and imagined. Chester refused to see that things were changing, although he seemed pleased enough with the decision to move. He had thrown himself into Wystan's squabble with Giocondo, which became increasingly unpleasant. Giocondo had become dissatisfied with his job as houseboy/general factotum. He tried painting, but discovered that something more than an 'artistic temperament' was needed for success. Then he planned to open a *pensione* in Sant'Angelo. That required capital. The advice he took, probably from his American brother-in-law, was hardly wise. Wystan had sent him a cheque to pay for household expenses; instead of 60,000 lire, Wystan made a mistake and sent a cheque for 600,000 (in those days the difference between $100 and $1,000, and a considerable sum when a house could be purchased for $2,000). Wystan discovered his error and airmailed the proper amount, telling Giocondo to destroy the first cheque. Giocondo presented both cheques to the bank. It was madness to think he could get away with it. Forio had only one bank – and that a new arrival – so the clerks knew everyone's account and regular transactions. Besides, there wasn't enough money in Wystan's account to cover both cheques. Giocondo and friend then spread the story that the larger cheque reflected 'services rendered'. That was patently absurd as well as vicious. Neither Wystan nor Chester would have sex with anyone so closely connected to their communal life. They had a very strict code governing sexual behaviour – although the rules were wellnigh incomprehensible to outsiders.

Had they been halcyon days? Less so than in memory, I suspect. But oh, the memories are lovely! The talk, the laughter, the mind-stretching, the becoming oneself, or better than oneself. Not just funnier or cleverer but actually better. It was wonderful!

How did the friendship with Wystan begin? Longstanding friendship can be sustained by shared memories or just by habit (I have often wondered about 'habits': do we invent them? how do we think them up?) but new ones need some impetus. It was so natural, a friendship without thought or strategy – like a blood relationship, with the added blessing of being non-exclusive and non-possessive. It was, as Wystan wrote, a 'concern for one another absent or present'. Something wonderfully soothing that one slipped into and never slipped out of. After all, there is no such thing as an unrequited friendship.

'You were in love with Auden, weren't you?' an aggressive *grande dame* asked me years later. This was Joan Haslip, for many years an arbiter of Anglo-Florentine society. This was a question no one who had ever seen us together would have asked. I laughed my denial; it seemed such a preposterous question. I most decidedly never went or wanted to go to bed with him. Is that an answer? *Is* there such a thing as a completely non-physical love? Or a completely physical love for that matter? I wonder.

Wystan did ask me to marry him, though – walking home from Neil Little's after a dinner party, both of us quite boozy. When he suggested it, I stopped in my tracks. He assured me he meant it seriously, so that we could have a son and name him Chester. All I would say was 'WYSTAN!', which seemed somehow to settle things; we walked the rest of the way home singing songs from *Pal Joey*. 'Barkis,' Wystan said the next day (Dickens once again a useful shorthand), so I had not dreamed it; with that he felt honour (his and mine) was saved and it was never mentioned again.

What would a distinguished middle-aged homosexual writer want with a giddy young woman? I was certainly no intellectual, I was aggressively heterosexual; we had practically no vices in common. But from the beginning I never doubted Wystan's affection. Chester's, yes; but never Wystan's. That made me seek Chester's approval but not bother about Wystan's. It is hard to explain, even to myself, what this period in our lives meant. Not to be bound or fixed, either sexually or socially, is wonderfully liberating. This suspended innocence couldn't last, but the magic can still be remembered.

One night at The Caffè Wystan said that to him the most difficult commandment to obey was 'Love thy neighbour'. This started a lengthy discussion involving tradition, literary sources and history until I asked, 'Wystan, just who is your neighbour?' Everyone had an answer to that question, and we had arrived at 'all humanity' when Wystan answered, 'Anyone who needs you.' Being with Wystan was like playing tennis with a superior player; it improved your game.

Wystan and I, unlike Chester, chose never to go back to Ischia. I felt rather like the protagonist in *The Age of Innocence* who sat on a park bench and sent his son up to see his old love. I didn't want to diminish the memories. Wystan was ready to move on, and if that meant not remembering why 'one had been happy', well, so be it.

# PART II
# Kirchstetten

In June 1957 Wystan won the Italian Lincei Literary Prize for lifetime achievement. The 20,000,000 lire (then about 32,000 dollars) was the largest amount of money he ever possessed. He was able, at last, to buy Chester and himself a house. (It was always 'our' house. At times Wystan referred to 'my' land but never to 'my' house.) Ischia by 1957 had become to Wystan a place 'where nothing really important can happen', the social changes bothered him too. 'Goodbye to the Mezzogiorno' had been in the making for quite some time so it was inevitable that he go north to 'a climate where it is a pleasure to walk', to live among 'those who mean by a life a *Bildungsroman*'.

He bought the Kirchstetten house in October 1957, I think. His letter to me of the 10th describing the place was longer than usual, and uncharacteristically filled with adjectives. A card from Chester shortly afterwards was equally enthusiastic. A certain amount of work was necessary and they didn't move in until the spring of 1959.

Chester took to Kirchstetten. He planted a vegetable garden, grew morning glories and seemed content, when Wystan went to New York, with just the company of a radio that reached the Third Programme of the Italian RAI and played opera most of the day. A letter from Chester that first spring (dated April 18th) told me, 'Here I am in Central Europe brooding on and over my ill-gotten property, when I should be contemplating my navel, or at least our navy. As a matter of pure fact I'm feeling absolutely wonderful; it's almost half-past nine and that's way past my usual bedtime here in the country. I do admit I took a benzedrine capsule this morning (it spreads its action over the day) but that was just to jolt myself out of this bucolic pipe-dream I've been living quite happily in. Moo!' The miracle seemed in the making. I wrote to Wystan, who was so delighted he rang me from New York to comment and ask what I thought he should do. 'Nothing,' I said, and he sounded relieved.

Shortly after they had settled in, I paid my first visit to Kirchstetten in 1959. I was their second house guest, the first was our old friend from Ischia, Neil Little. (I particularly remember because Neil had written so cleverly in the newly acquired guest-book and all I could write was 'love'.) From then on I never missed a summer visit. After John and I were married in 1961 he, my daughter and, after his birth in 1965, our son came with me. The Visit became a fixture, almost a necessity in the life of both households. We saw one another fairly often in England, in New York and in Florence but The Visit was different. That was family, family at home, which was extremely important to Wystan. He greatly loved his brother John and all of John's family but he was greedy for more. We helped. I have never understood why Chester resisted this need. John says it was self-preservation that he – Chester – could and would be almost everything – companion, cook, collaborator – but wouldn't, couldn't, allow himself to be absorbed into The Family.

A daily routine was soon worked out, and the first years in Kirchstetten were rewarding. There was a pleasant friendship with the local Roman Catholic priest, Father Lustkandle; Wystan never missed a Sunday service. Chester – like the socialist husbands of Italian countrywomen – waited outside. 'Outside' was Frau Biba's inn nearby, where over a beer and a sandwich he worked on the morning's crossword and waited for Wystan. He entered the church only for the funeral, which was a shame, as the drama and Hollywoodiana of the Mass would have appealed to him.

Wystan threw himself into community activities, attended school meetings, delivered speeches, pondered road building problems, became a useful as well as a distinguished citizen. Austrian villagers proved to be no more grateful than certain literary critics – those of the 'carpet slipper school' who keep telling their readers how dirty the apartment at St Mark's Place was, and who seem to think that Wystan's eccentricities were more important than his achievements.

Much thought and care and joy went into the planning of what was to be the rest of their lives. Setting up the American kitchen with all its new equipment: an infra-red grill; a gloriously grand deep freeze; French casseroles; a bread slicer that popped up unexpectedly out of a drawer; rows of knives for trimming, slicing, carving, chopping, a *batterie de cuisine* that would have satisfied Elizabeth David. Wystan's 'cave', isolated from the rest of the house and reached by an unpainted outside wooden staircase, was sparsely, though carefully, furnished; it was there that 'silence is turned into objects'. Seeing him go either up or down those rickety stairs was a lesson in humility, at least to me.

I first arrived at Kirchstetten at around ten-thirty at night on the train from Munich. Wystan and Chester drove over to the neighbouring town of St Pölten in the Volkswagen to fetch me. The German word for duty sounds like 'afflict' and that is what Wystan was muttering about the hour. Chester and I sat up late and gossiped – we hadn't seen each other in months, not since New York. There was the usual Chester sentimentality and romanticism about his latest love. I tried to be sympathetic.

The next morning brought the tour: house, garden and village. My first introduction was to Emma and Josef Eiermann, the housekeeper and her brother. Josef was shyly polite, Emma was correct. Wystan and Chester had already created their myths about the place. There was a spot on the hill coming up from the railway station where the telegraph wires began to hum, which denoted 'home'. Their private language had been enriched by things like calling the plate-warmer 'apple'. I can't remember why, only that it amused both of them.

Wystan loved the German language, and Chester with his remarkable ear soon spoke it colloquially and rapidly. When they first came to Austria he spoke only Pidgin Deutsch but after a month or so of intense study and speaking English only to the cat he was chatting away, using Neapolitan gestures as he spoke. Shortly after his arrival he wrote: 'The only mother tongue I managed was in the Vienese (SP?) shops. There I just marched in and announced that I wanted someone who spoke a white-folk's language. They always had someone (I didn't, but I must suppress that terrible bitterness, mustn't I?) So I gaily bought casseroles and onion choppers and frying pans. Oh, it was gay! Alas, I also thought I could squeeze in a little culture. However, since my diet, casual as it is, I just couldn't squeeze in Tebaldi's Tosca, and that seemed the main Kultur-staple at the time. I did rest a very jaundiced eye on some fotos of the gal. Who does her make-up? She looked like a Korean horse; and it's not too long ago that I did see La Divina (my Greek sister) in Tosca-ola. So I hustled my sagging buttocks back to the country and here I've been sitting on them ever since.'

His letters in those first years were more and more filled with domestic news: 'The weather is pleasant enough now, and we've bought lovely garden furniture to lounge in and enjoy, thumbing our noses (when we aren't scratching our hands) at the dear little midges. Who also enjoy the weather. Not being Schweizers we slap our way through the natural world and don't mind it all that much. But Pete Butorac who was here, found it too much after 18 insectless months working in Greenland; and so I'm sure would Charles have, who ALWAYS seems to break out in welts whenever he visits us, either here or back in Ischia.'

The Charles mentioned was Charles Heiliman, a talented designer and close friend whose early death from a heart condition was a severe blow to Chester. I have never met Pete Butorac who was at one time a tenant (only) at St Mark's Place: Anne and Irving saw him whenever possible.

Chester's delight continued and he urged me to visit often: 'It really is quite lovely. Birds sing so pretty-like. Not like those damn Florentine Nightingales (or is it Florence Nightingales?) that keep you awake all night waiting for another Keats to set them to verse; these birds are sunlight birds. At night all is still here except for the faint moans of horny Americans dreaming of khaki-colored eclairs. (On the radio Norina has just screamed: "Un uomo! Un uomo!") and I'll take you to St Pölten, which I can only describe as the Lucca of the north. WOW! But I found it rather scary and foreign, so I just stayed long enough to buy some Stock Weinbrand. I guess I'm over sensitive. Needless to say, though, I intend to swallow my pride (no jokes please) and bumble through the town in my miserable German rather soon. Oh Vienna's "fun", lots, but I do like discovering new blood, if "blood" is the word I'm groping for. You notice, don't you, that I'm keeping back any gossip I might have – damn little – just so we'll have LOTS to talk about when we meet. And soon, soon. I've gone on for so long and Stella Stock is beginning to make her effect, the bitch – So love and kisses to you and Lisa and the conte and just an extra bit to you from – Ljuba Librettista.'

In deference to his new surroundings he had bought the most outrageous pair of lederhosen, soft white leather with delicate blue stitching. He had been visited in a dream by his beloved grandmother and had promised her that this was at last 'home'. Wystan discussed his happiness with the cats and the morning glories.

When I first visited Kirchstetten, Wystan felt I should be introduced to Vienna. As I had only spent two days there and had seen only the Staatsoper and the Kunsthistorisches Museum, he felt it his duty to further my education. Our first stop was Schönbrunn. It was also almost my first experience of Wystan as a chauffeur. He had no car in Ischia, a disastrous experience with a Vespa motor scooter having nearly cost him the use of one eye. The night I arrived in St Pölten I was too excited to notice his driving, and at that hour in the Austrian countryside there was no one else on the road. Driving into Vienna was quite different: I was pleased to note that Schönbrunn was on 'their' side of Vienna so there was no heavy city traffic. Chester, who did not drive, was oblivious to the danger and fortunately I am not a nervous passenger, usually. Anyway, we had a trot through the palace and a canter through the gardens. Wystan showed me around with a proprietorial air; he apologized that one of the ceramic stoves was dusty. Chester said he could never have been a happy Habsburg as he looked sallow in yellow. It was fun but I couldn't help saying that, wonderful as it all was, 'it isn't me.' They both laughed, as each had said the same thing the last time they had visited.

That was the first in a series of outings that continued until the last two years. After that first year there was a regular and quite democratic consultation before any decision was made. A strict set of rules was devised – at least one outing a visit, a trip to Vienna for shopping and a quick bite didn't count, and we had to go further than Neulengbach. No outings at all until a full morning's work had been put in. The actual day was reserved when we arrived, the venue had usually been decided by letter. The preparations were intense. Wystan collected maps, studied them carefully, and discussed them at length; John and I, who often drove really long distances, laughed about it, but only in the privacy of our room.

We had some lovely times. One golden day we went in two cars, with Lisa and two friends, to Melk. Then, after visiting the monastery, we put the young on a Danube boat, together with Chester's friend Yannis, and we four drove slowly along the Danube to meet them at Krems. A longer boat ride would have been welcomed but Chester couldn't resist the Melk/

Krems idea. As we drove along the banks of the Danube we stopped frequently to have a beer or just to gaze at the vineyards that spilled down the steep hillsides. At one such stop Wystan began to sing German songs; even Chester fell silent.

In 1959 something happened between the two of them. It came as such a surprise that I was still trying to figure it out when the crisis was over. Hans Henze arrived in Kirchstetten the first week in August (I had visited in July) to discuss the libretto for his opera *Elegy for Young Lovers*. Wystan and Chester were enthusiastic, and Chester wrote to me 'it's getting dippier by the minute' and Wystan that he was cross at having to return to New York 'just as the fun was starting'. Then out of the blue came a card from Chester saying that he was 'running away from home'. This was followed by a cryptic telegram saying, 'For the moment treachery is prospering, much to my disappointment.' The telegram came from Lisbon with no indication of a return address. September 29th brought a vivaciously tinted postcard from Algarve saying, 'Algarve offers everything price-wise that Tuscany does not. All my desiderata are here, house, terrace, fireplace, devoted slaves, company (of a sort). But I don't really want to live here! It is pretty but monumentally dull! I may confuse the issue and go back to Austria.' Whatever the trouble was, it passed, and in the autumn Chester was back in Kirchstetten hard at work on *Elegy*.

All meals in Kirchstetten were taken in the dining area of the largest room in the house. There was a built-in bench along the wall, a rectangular table and spindly-legged alpine chairs. Wystan was the only one with a permanent place at the end of the table, facing the window, where there was a volume of the *OED* for him to sit on. The table and chairs were of shiny blond wood with cushions upholstered in a plaid that blended uncomfortably with the plaid used for the curtains. Above the bench was a painting on glass of a chubby Neapolitan Christ Child. The painting, whose value was purely sentimental, was a gift from Hans Henze. Neither Wystan nor Chester had much of what, for want of a better expression, is called visual sense. There were drawings or prints of taste, but they had been chosen for literary reasons: a print of the Munch head of Strauss, a wonderful drawing of Stravinsky by Don Bachardy, and what seemed to us a banal painting of the Mediterranean seen through an open window. The painting we liked best, illustrating an Indian myth, was done by John Auden's wife Sheila, herself an Indian. At first Wystan gave it only slight attention, although praising Sheila, of whom he was very fond. Then he read V. S. Naipaul's first book on India and the painting was properly appreciated. The most prominent object in the room was a handsome ceramic stove that we never saw functioning.

The room itself was large and almost square with small, high casement windows, satisfying Wystan's wish to look out without being observed. The far left-hand corner was the dining area, the far right, which also had a built-in bench and a smaller but equally ugly table, was for cocktails and before dinner conversation. There were letters, magazines, books and papers everywhere – on the tables, on the chairs, on the floor, on the stove. The floor was of local wood and smelled of the beeswax that Frau Eiermann applied weekly. After her death the next housekeeper let the floor go and I didn't smell the wax again until the day of Wystan's funeral, when three village ladies had come in to polish up for the event.

Tea was served outside on a round white table with a hole in the centre for an umbrella. This, together with several comfortable but hideous, glistening chairs, made up the outside furniture, bought from a shop which also sold garden sculpture, a temptation that Chester resisted with difficulty.

Tea outside, a Campari or vermouth before lunch, but cocktails, never. They were always served inside, heat or no heat. With the arrival of the deep-freeze the Martinis took on a new dimension and for some reason the gin was replaced by vodka, the olives by pickled onions. The glasses were chilled there, the vermouth was kept there, so was the vodka: as no ice was necessary there was no dilution. Only two were allowed: one at six-thirty, one at seven; dinner was seven-thirty sharp. After the first year or so they began to cheat (I'm not sure which one, as each blamed the other), and the glasses seemed to get bigger with each visit, though the cocktail routine was rigorously enforced. The first Martini, served promptly at six-thirty, allowed John and Wystan a half-hour together to talk about theology and money, while Lisa and I stayed in the kitchen with Chester to put the finishing touches to the night's dinner. With the second Martini we emerged, and the talk became more general. We talked about sex only after dinner; it was bad form during the day, but at night, sitting around the table drinking the foul Valpolicella that seemed made especially for the Austrian market and for which Wystan had developed a tolerance, anything could be discussed, and was. 'I'm queerer than you are,' said Wystan to Chester. 'Don't give yourself airs,' was Chester's reply, 'at least I'm pure.' Wystan had indeed slept with women, besides Rhoda Jaffe with whom he had a serious affair in 1946. I learned this from Chester, who accented the 'serious' although it was he who chose the expensive handbag Wystan bought Rhoda for her birthday. When I asked him if he had gone to bed with the handsome German/American woman who had followed him to Ischia in 1952 (or was it 1953?), 'my dear, she insisted,' he said. She had the distinction of being the last woman to make it to his bed. Asked about the difference he felt in making love to men or women, he said he could feel physical attraction for women but love only for men.

We all talked about ourselves, our quirks, our secrets. I remember once mentioning a foolish thing I had done as a child, which had left me with an embarrassing memory – the kind of thing one can say only after too much food, too much wine and too little control – and it was taken seriously, examined and explained. Nothing was too trivial if it had actually happened. Wystan always knew if one was lying.

Wystan tried out ideas in conversation and Chester tried out words. Chester was a brilliant performer; Wystan was dismal. Chester told Jewish stories that went on and on and were hilarious. Wystan tried to repeat them, with calamitous results. The accent was off, the timing was abysmal, and he often gave the punch-line away. Chester and I would egg him on, naughtily. One year there was a book called *The Joys of Yiddish* and each took turns in reading from it. It was two different books that way – each amusing in its own fashion. Chester had a large repertoire of stories, Italian (Neapolitan, that is) and Greek as well as Jewish. Strangely, I never heard an Austrian or German joke. He loved old movies – also a passion of mine – the worse the better. One of his best performances was from a dreadful old film about Mme du Barry in which he played both the Norma Talmadge and the Conrad Nagel parts. He was shamelessly sentimental when, after careful preparation, he brought his listeners to the final line of an Olivia de Havilland film about mother-love (*To Each his Own*). His eyes would fill with tears as he said, 'This is our dance . . . Mother.' He performed with perfect timing and exaggerated but delicate and memorable gestures. But it was Wystan who demanded to play an elephant when he, four-year-old Lisa and I pranced and danced to a record playing the Triumphal March from *Aida*. 'This,' said Wystan, 'is grand opera and happiness', though he knew full well that orgy is not happiness.

In 1959 my Italian marriage was rocky and I was having a feeble affair with an American academic called Tom. That July he followed me to Austria. Until I married John I always made the Austrian visit alone. A telegram announcing Tom's arrival in Vienna on Monday, and asking for a meeting the next day, arrived in Kirchstetten on Tuesday afternoon. Chester was intrigued, so he and I decided to go to Vienna on Wednesday to see if we could find him. We did, and there was Tom at the Mozart Café, quite attractive, wearing the self-confidence of someone 'highly respected in his field', with that think-tank look that American academics seem to acquire. Dressed with studied casualness, he exuded pure essence of California.

We brought him back to Kirchstetten in time for one of Chester's wonderful meals, during which he asked for salt. This would have been passable if he hadn't begun to talk 'seriously'. He asked Wystan if there was anything he had done in his life that would send him to Hell. Wystan replied, 'I should leave that to higher authorities.' Instead of catching the tone, this launched Tom on a discussion of comparative religion, a subject Wystan usually enjoyed. He managed to make it boring, and when he thundered against the Koran, saying, 'Give me the Old Testament any day!' and Chester replied 'We did' and he didn't laugh – I knew it was all over. That night he slept on a sagging divan at Frau Biba's inn, and it was a gummy-eyed, disgruntled man I met for coffee *mit schlag* in the morning. I thought I had tactfully explained why it was impossible that I join him in Vienna, but I must have done it badly. He muttered something about not wanting to sleep with all three of us. His field was psychology; his self-confidence monumental; his understanding zilch – and I should have known better. Wystan said to me the next day, 'My dear, you couldn't have thought seriously about him; just imagine the conversation at breakfast.'

I think it was the following year that Chester got the sausage-making machine. It was an event. Frau Ei looked at it with unconcealed scorn. Wystan said he expected it to save a great deal of money. Chester and I laboured to follow the instructions for setting it up. Unfortunately it arrived on the scene before John did. He would have made short work of what for us was a damnably difficult job. The grand inauguration took place three days after its arrival. The first batch hardly met Wystan's requirements; they were made of chicken breasts and truffles. The second batch had more economical ingredients, but we made a miscalculation and the quantities were so vast that Chester and I were up until one o'clock in the morning finishing the casings. The next morning Wystan found a necklace of sausages hanging above his place at the table. Below them we had written 'This is a result of work, not labour'. It had seemed funny at one in the morning. Like so many things in Kirchstetten, this led to other thoughts. That evening Wystan said, half-seriously, that we had just given him proof that preparing food and cooking was an art not a craft. Had we been craftsmen, instead of artists, we would have known what the end-product would be.

One summer, either 1959 or 1960, I agreed to teach Chester to drive the Volkswagen. He had tried learning with Wystan, but, not surprisingly, that hadn't worked. 'I'm only doing it to please – no, to show Wystan,' Chester said. Not a promising start. However, the first three lessons went well and Chester enjoyed mastering the car. We went fairly far afield, to give him confidence and keep him from getting bored. It was on the fourth time out that we ran into trouble. We had been on the road for over two hours when we stopped briefly at a *gasthaus* where I had a beer and Chester coffee. He ordered it proudly, to underline his new responsibility as a driver. We spent quite a bit of time talking about ourselves; he about the direction his life was taking. Then back into the car for the drive home.

We were nearly at the railway station which signalled 'home', and were busy congratulating each other, when Chester in a dramatic display of confidence, took the corner too fast, skidded on the gravel, panicked, lost control, and ran into two parked cars on one side of the road, bounced off them and ran into a parked motorcycle on the other side. We were both shaken. There was no serious damage, but it was obvious that repairs would be expensive. Chester was frightened and defiant; I thought of myself at fourteen when I had smashed

1 W. H. Auden in downtown Florence, 1956.

2 Chester Kallman (right) on the ferry to Ischia.

3 Chester, Bill Smith and Thekla Clark waiting for the boat in Forio. In the foreground is Wystan's dog, Mosè.

4 Irving Weiss and Wystan outside Maria's Caffè.

5 Wystan's photograph of Lisa on the beach at San Francesco,
near Forio.

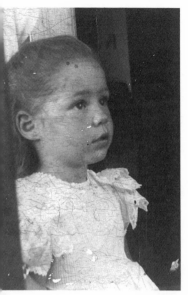

6  Auden's photograph of Lisa.

7  Wystan on the terrace fiddling with his camera.

8  Simon's christening party (Chester at left), described on page 65.

9 Wystan with his sister-in-law Sheila at Anita's wedding, Terzano, 1968.

10 Chester (right) with the bride and groom.

11 John Clark, Chester, Thekla, Kosta the first, Wystan – Piazzale
Michelangelo, Florence, 1965.

12 Wystan at the Clarks' house in Florence.

13 Chester and an unknown Evzone.

14 Chester and Wystan at Kirchstetten.

15 Chester and friend on the Acropolis. The text of Chester's
postcard appears on page 57.

my father's car. Chester stopped a local man on a motorcycle and asked him to take a message to Wystan. I couldn't understand what he said, but it was effective, as Wystan came striding along in record time. His face showed such relief when he saw us on our feet that I wondered just what the message had been. The first thing he said was, 'Quite an achievement.' Chester relaxed and we all laughed, rather too loudly.

Lisa and I spent the Christmas of 1959 in Oklahoma with my parents. The trip was also a trial separation from Alberto. I found I liked the situation and made it permanent. The scheduled visit of three weeks turned into a stay of over three months, and we didn't return to Florence until March 1960. Two days after our return my friend Maria Teresa Cini invited me to dinner to meet John Clark. The attraction was certainly there and we had a lovely time, although we rowed almost immediately. He had been reading (and admiring) *The Naked Lunch*. We began seeing quite a bit of each other. However, there was another candidate and John seemed in no hurry. Things stumbled along inconclusively until May, when I was summoned back to Oklahoma to be with my mother. After a blessed remission from cancer she suffered a stroke which proved fatal. She was sitting with her sister when she felt a paralysis in her arm. 'Oh, oh, oh,' she sighed, and then turned to her sister and said, 'Tell Jimmy [my father] it's been grand', before losing consciousness. She was in the hospital, motionless, when I arrived and she died on the morning of the following day.

When I got back to Florence there were letters from both Wystan and Chester. They urged me to come to Kirchstetten as soon as possible, which I did. They were tender with me, and I learned that grief can be shared, at least in part. Chester was 'stunned' (his word) by my mother's death, as though he had expected his wishes to heal her. His mourning was genuine, his grief disturbing. Wystan was far more realistic and, truthfully, more comforting. Towards the end of the visit I told them about the 'two candidates'. Chester was non-committal and Wystan admonished, 'No more false starts.' He was right, of course, and I went home knowing, at last, what I wanted. That was June. By December John was also convinced.

February 11th was until recently an Italian holiday, celebrating Mussolini's Concordat between Church and State. For practical, not political, reasons John and I chose that date for our wedding in 1961 at St James' American church in Florence.

We began our married life – together with Lisa, Liliana (our Tuscan 'Tituta'), one dog, two cats and a tank of tropical fish – in a house on Via Ugo Foscolo, rented from our friend Luigino Franchetti. In October 1962 Chester came to stay with us there; he came alone. That in itself was unusual, as he seldom travelled without Wystan and/or a boyfriend. He came to work on a project that John had devised for a children's book with music and projected slides. Chester was writing the poems to accompany the sophisticated drawings; the music was by the American composer Francis Thorne. ('Many thanks for the copies of Chester's verse,' wrote Wystan. 'They seem to me to be awfully good. To write poems for children without being arch is fiendishly difficult, but he has managed it.') The verses celebrated a trip to the circus, and I include one of the poems here:

*Mister Stephen Mackeever, Juggler*

Juggling Steve
          (Mister Mackeever)
Weave
    your cover of a hover ever over
Round your head like a hollow halo –
                HELLO!

On you go
With right hand
        left hand

Each a deft hand,
Ev-er-y globe aglow –
Up
   and about and down and across the flow,
                      so
Light
    and
Ready to leave
Again
   then again up:
           Steve
Achieving
Rainbow whirlwinds of getting and giving
Hard to believe
NEVER
   too early or late:
Oh
  great
Mackeever, heaver, retriever,
Watching your
      catching for
           love of dispatching more,
I've a fever!
      VIVA
Juggling Steve (a
      Mister Mackeever).

Originally planned as a two to three week visit, such was the pleasure Chester took in the project and the delight we took in his company that the stay stretched to over two months. In all that time he only slipped into town once. He developed a work routine and kept to it as rigidly as Wystan kept to his.

Our house in Via Ugo Foscolo was a square, newly converted farmhouse, neither imaginative nor particularly attractive but set in a handsome, isolated olive grove. At the front of the house was the *aia*, a flat, flagstoned space originally used for threshing grain. There Chester would take his morning coffee and his work in fine weather. I was recovering from a miscarriage, and he was happily solicitous for me. We spent a great deal of time together. He helped with the shopping and often went into the kitchen, where he had become a great favourite with Liliana. She, as a good Tuscan, was amused by Chester's Italian with its strong Neapolitan accent. And as a good Tuscan she deplored his unmarried state; he should share all that wealth, she maintained.

We read, we gossiped, we listened to records, we cooked, we pickled and preserved until we filled the larder, we worried about Lisa and discussed her future, endlessly. Chester loved reading aloud which he did wonderfully well in a rich, juicy baritone; on that visit he was especially keen on James Merrill's poetry and Nabokov's short stories, so I got healthy doses of each. Chester confessed that he had never felt so masculine, and so cared for, in all his life. Besides the children's songs, he was working on his own poetry, and this gave him great satisfaction. Nights we would have friends in to dinner, go out, or just sit around the table laughing or talking until one of us drooped. Weekends, under John's guidance, we explored Tuscany. John was impressed with Chester's understanding and enthusiasm; I was equally impressed by his energy, stamina and constancy. The visit was uneventful except that I gained eight pounds from Chester's cooking and he lost almost an equal amount by cutting down on the drink.

As was to be expected, Chester eventually became restless, 'itchy', he said. We were sorry when the 'itch' became insistent; Chester, I think, sorriest of all. I took him to the railway station, and there was regret on both sides. However, once there, he managed to get himself a seat in what looked like a troop train and was soon in conversation with a handsome 'Alpino', a soldier from an Alpine regiment, whose peaked hat with its black feather was a feature of the deliciously naughty clerihew he sent us. Chester tried to keep his emotions in check with camp humour; looking through old letters one sees how often he succeeded. A card with a photograph of Chester and friend announcing true love went: 'A view from the Acropolis Hill or the answer to that nagging question "But what did you *see*, Mr Kallman, while you were in Greece; and just what did you *do*?" Well I was miserable and loved every minute of it. Isn't the landscape divine? More later (including the five poems so far). About the landscape. What else? *E per tutta la vita.* Love, love, love. C.'

It was with Wystan and Chester that we got into the habit of sitting around the dinner table long after the meal was over, a habit we continue still with close friends, in memory of those evenings in Kirchstetten. Sometimes after dinner Chester would put on a record or two (the choice was always his) but it was mainly talk: frivolous, wide-ranging, truthful, unvarnished and plain. Evening conversations were a testing ground for new ideas. When the ideas got out of hand, as they sometimes did, Wystan could be teased, cajoled or shamed out of them. Once he made some drastic statement that perpetrators of certain animal experiments should be gassed, and Chester turned on him saying, 'You of all people can't use language that way!' His garumphed apology, though scarcely audible, was genuine. He knew he had gone too far, and was grateful for a way out.

He had a complicated theory about time and space and their genders. Time, he insisted, was masculine because of its mathematical organization and men, while they could neglect their appearance as that was spatial, must always be punctual. Space, as it was a sense of place, was feminine and it didn't matter if women were late for appointments. 'Really, Wystan,' I said, 'you've obviously never been pregnant!' That must have worked, since that particular theory was never discussed again, so far as I know.

Wonderful games were begun around the table after dinner. 'Paradise or Eden', 'the name game', 'boring or a bore', and many others which are now in print. Wystan was full of theories; some less than wise, there were so many. John is also an idea man, so I have first-hand experience. Neither Chester nor I were idea people, so we sat back and applauded when possible or exploded when necessary. Wystan enjoyed devising questionnaires that he claimed to be revealing. For example, had one been a contemporary and friend of one's parents and each had come to you in turn and asked if he or she should marry the other, what would you have said? I asked if he had ever had a positive answer and when he said 'Never' we all laughed.

One of Wystan's theories was that no true artist died before he had said 'what he had to say'. The moment Wystan mentioned this particular theory he was jumped upon by listeners screeching, 'What about Mozart?', or other short-lived geniuses. He went on to qualify the statement by saying that none of them (Mozart, Masaccio, Shelley, etc) had left any evidence that he was moving on to something new. The only exception was Keats, as Wystan felt that in the last letters there was an indication of new ideas and development. It was not a popular theory, but that never stopped Wystan. I suppose he was trying to tell us something; it was a late theory, late in his life that is, and he was tired.

John and Wystan would often sit and throw ideas back and forth. Chester and I sat on the sidelines, rather like spectators at a tennis match. Mentioning this to Chester he said to me, 'Instead of a tennis ball I think of it as a shuttlecock.' I remember once a discussion about the relative merits of jewels or furs as gifts to the beloved. An academic discussion if ever there was one, but argued with extreme seriousness.

The talk was continuous and exhilarating. John called it 'a challenge for the mind, a nourishment for the spirit'. The ideas were mostly Wystan's but he welcomed any additions or embroidery. One particularly wine-soaked evening he and John mused about what they would have said and done had they been present at the Crucifixion. Chester was inclined to belittle Wystan's religion. He had his own set of deities which consisted of his grandmother, Rose, and later his dead Greek friend, Yannis. He, like Wystan, needed 'the companionship of our good dead'. He wrote a tender poem about Rose in her narrow bed and a heartfelt one about Yannis.

Pairs of couples who spend a great deal of time together often find themselves divided in tastes and ideas, rather like choosing sides. One such issue with us was climate. When it rained in Kirchstetten Wystan purred like a huge leathery cat and Chester and I fretted. John, like Wystan, loves fog and mist and Romantic landscapes; Chester and I longed for the sun and the sea. We were teased by the damp pair, who claimed the drip of water from the trees was a pure celestial sound. All we could hear were the raspberries rotting, the morning glories complaining and the mildew forming. One evening when we opened the front door the mist actually came into the room, to the delight of some and the horror of others.

Wystan loved all church ritual and tolerated even the worst sermon. 'One can amuse oneself by counting heresies,' he said. His responses at Kirchstetten's church, where he sat upstairs by the organ, were louder than anyone else's. He was annoyed when Father Lustkandle allowed a bossy nun to lead the responses downstairs. It was intended as a help to the congregation, but Wystan took it as a challenge, as did the nun, and Sunday services left them both hoarse.

Although there were three inns in Kirchstetten Wystan and Chester went only to Frau Biba's. Relations were cordial, but Frau Biba never took the place of Maria. Wystan went most days at around eleven, after the shopping or church, and Chester went almost as often; but never at night. I noticed also that neither had any 'adventures' in the village; Chester never even flirted with the local youth. I wanted to ask if they had made a conscious decision about this but never had the courage, so I could only guess. Knowing them, I felt that had such a decision been made it would have required long and serious discussions: I only wish I could have been party to them.

The years and the visits to Kirchstetten all mix together in my mind. I remember the excitements, the passions, the *Black Like Me* year; the M. F. K. Fisher year. We all saved up for the summer. New ideas, books that we hoped the others hadn't read yet, concerts, operas or records we had heard, funny stories and, of course, gossip. There would often be one special subject per summer. Neither John nor I had read *Black Like Me* or M. F. K. Fisher but we brought in exchange Pasolini's *Accattone* and records of the ill-fated soprano Anita Cerquetti. Then there was the first teenage year. John and I brought Lisa, aged twelve, and two young boys, aged fourteen, with us for the annual Visit. There wasn't room at the house so the young bedded with a local family nearby. Lisa to this day recalls the particular smell of Austrian loos with horror. Wystan's was no exception. There were always books carefully chosen to serve a rather special purpose. John one year discovered the ideal book to pee by – Wystan and Louis Kronenberger's *Aphorisms*, and it was from then on given pride of place. One of the boys managed to do something to the lock of the lavatory door and no one could get in or out. 'This,' said Wystan, 'is serious, a man locked out of his own loo.' 'And in the prime of life,' said Chester. John was hoisted up through a small outside window and somehow managed to pick the lock and throw open the door, to cheers from the rest of us assembled on the outside. The pleasure that Wystan took from this exploit seemed to me excessive, but then I was used to household dramas. All was forgiven the teenager when he wrote in the guest-book. For Chester it was 'They say you're a poet guy / Well take another look / Poets aren't so special / I prefer you as a cook.' For Wystan 'Poets like you are hard to find / If you're not the best around / You're just a little behind.' To Wystan's further delight one of the boys (Benedict Fitzgerald, son of our friends Robert and Sally) was Catholic and wanted to go to Confession before Mass on Sunday. He knew no German and Father Lustkandle knew neither English nor Italian, so the confession was made in Latin. At the end of what must have been a pale recital, as Benedict was a gentle, well-loved older son, the priest ordered *'Drei Ave Marias'*. The whole thing gave Wystan such pleasure that he played cards with the young as a reward. No one particularly enjoyed the game but it was a gesture. John and I noticed that whenever we talked about our children Wystan reached for his cats.

There was another, less amusing, household crisis that year. Chester and I decided that the young should do the washing-up, which seemed logical since there were so many dishes. Frau Ei, the gaunt, wispy-haired housekeeper, took offence; Wystan said 'umbrage'. Chester's kitchen, celebrated though it was, was a chaotic jumble of the last meal's leftovers and the next one's preparations. When John and I came down in the morning we hurried past the kitchen, with lowered heads and averted eyes, into the living room for coffee. No matter how quickly we passed, the strong smell of beautifully elaborate stale dishes pursued us. Chester outdid himself with all those healthy teenage appetites. It brought out the Jewish mother in him. One evening he swore that the kitchen was filled with the smell of Rose's chopped liver, although he was cooking something quite different. It was, he insisted, her blessing. Chopped liver as the odour of sanctity appealed to me greatly. Anyway, Frau Ei refused to enter the kitchen the entire time we were there with the children. She felt that their presence at the kitchen sink was a criticism of her, as she had always done the washing-up. That is what she told John, who knew enough German to ask what was the matter. Another family conference was held, Wystan presiding, and after a lengthy discussion involving Teutonic tribal organization and 'the Czech's chance to be brutal', the matter was wisely dropped. Frau Ei (her Christian name was Emma, but it was never used) lived with her brother, Josef, in a tiny house in the garden. No one else ever entered the house; all conversation was carried on through the window. They were Sudetenland German refugees, expelled from the Czech Republic after the Second World War, who had never made friends in the village. I never learned who was the elder, as they looked like twins. Josef's death made Frau Ei more silent than ever. She seemed to like John and Chester, and deferred to Wystan but I saw her smile only when we brought Simon as an infant to stay. She distrusted all Greeks. If one of Chester's friends was out in the garden alone the window curtains in her little house moved constantly. She died quietly, suddenly, and I'm afraid, alone, as Wystan and Chester were in New York.

She was succeeded by a bustling, garrulous, waistless Austrian whom none of us ever warmed to and who was named 'La D' for *Direttissima*, an Italian train (*Direttissimo*) that makes a great noise and promise of speed but takes for ever to arrive anywhere. She was a good soul but never seemed quite right for the place, like dear, strange Frau Ei.

Keeping the house in order was a thankless task. Since the housekeeper didn't know which books and papers could be touched, nothing was ever tidied up or put away. When we arrived, I would have a session with Chester putting things away, and even throwing out old newspapers – the unfinished crosswords had been kept in the hope that some-one could finish them. (As a matter of principle the answers in the next day's paper were not checked unless all the spaces had been filled in.)

The day began early in Kirchstetten. John and I were down-stairs shortly after seven but we were never the first. Yannis and the young got up later, but we four always breakfasted together. We slept with the door open, and the sound of the electric beater whipping the morning *schlag* was our alarm clock. There was a huge electric percolator, brought from New York, and it was refilled at least once. 'Good mornings' were polite, but real talk began only after the second cup of that boiling hot but weak coffee that Chester insisted was healthier although far nastier than the Italian variety. Wystan, who had been groggier than everyone the night before and had staggered off to bed, was never blurry-eyed, never admitted to a headache or even found it necessary to clear his throat. He already had a cigarette when we appeared, and it wasn't his first. Plans were made, dreams, if any, were discussed (Chester and I were usually the ones who remembered), and last night's conversation punctuated. We underlined some things (those we liked), put question marks around others and closed parentheses when necessary. Amazing how many cigarettes, cups of coffee and words were consumed in that stretchable half-hour at breakfast.

There was an outside porch with morning glories growing up on strings – a tribute to Ischia. Wystan was cross one year when he found morning-glory seeds unavailable in New York. The young had been chewing them to get high. 'As you have probably read,' he wrote, 'because of the damned juvenile delinquents, it is no longer possible in America or England to buy Morning Glory seeds. If by any chance Italy is being anarchic and has them still on sale, could you be an angel and send a packet or two.' 'God bless Italia,' he wrote after I had sent him several packages. It was the kind of interruption in routine that irritated him. At Kirchstetten he would come out every morning after breakfast to count how many flowers were in bloom. 'I would,' wrote Chester in a poem '. . . Never arrange Summer / Without morning glories / To count upon daily.'

In the mornings Chester sat on the porch with a huge mug of iced coffee and his work. As the years passed the iced coffee changed to Ouzo but the routine was the same. They both showed us work in progress, but neither ever read his work to us. Once we were with Chester at the house of a friend, who read his poetry to us after dinner. 'Thank God Wystan wasn't here,' Chester said afterwards. 'He always thought the man came from a good family.'

*

Shortly after John and I were married and they had decided that John 'would very much do' they made it official one night at dinner. Wystan, as the elder, started to mumble something but was interrupted by Chester, who declared that they both felt Lisa was now in competent paternal hands. When they handed Lisa over to John it didn't mean they no longer took an interest in her. Wystan worried, of all things, about her success in taking examinations. 'Too important these days,' he said. He felt it was too tempting a substitute for learning. Wystan also worried about her lack of practicality. All my fault, he implied, as I had read her unsuitable books at crucial moments. Too much Dickens at the wrong time, hence her 'friend of the people' attitude that he found boring, and too much Scott, and the 'wrong' Tennyson, which accounted for her over-romantic taste in boys. Mothers, he insisted, should bring their daughters up on a strict diet of Jane Austen.

They both believed that our son Simon was conceived in the guest room at Kirchstetten. As a matter of fact he was conceived in the nearby woods since that summer (1964) was beastly hot. The guest room was airless, and with the windows open we heard the steady hum of the autobahn, so John and I spent more time, both day and night, in the friendly woods. We never told them the truth, which would have distressed Chester and amused Wystan. Chester, for all his sentimentality about women, was repulsed by heterosexual 'goings on'. We heterosexuals, protected by our superior numbers and generally accepted 'normalcy', find it difficult to believe that our habits can be distasteful to others. Chester pretended to be appalled by the young who travelled together before they were married, or perhaps it wasn't pretence. Wystan made no distinction between hetero- and homosexual morality and seemed severe and forgiving at the same time – rather like the Old and the New Testament mixed together. They both disliked any outward show of masculinity, and when John grew a moustache it took them ages to come round to it. The only thing they disliked more than a hairy youth was an effeminate one.

Wystan was fascinated by female anatomy and the whole process of birth. 'You are so fortunate to have all your reproductive organs inside you,' he said, 'not these ridiculous things I find attached to me as an afterthought.' He and I had long and detailed gynaecological discussions, but we forbore from having them at table after one night Chester screamed, 'Mercy!' I noticed then that both he and John had turned pale. I once accused Wystan of being envious of my womb. 'Not really,' he answered, 'only jealous.'

When, after two miscarriages, I became safely pregnant with Simon, he followed my progress as closely as my doctor. Looking through old letters I found one in which he warns me against 'the desire for self-perpetuation'. I wrote asking what he meant, and he answered, 'Many parents want children not as new persons but to prolong their own existence.'

Wystan, who was Simon's godfather, couldn't come to his christening in June 1965 so he sent Chester in his place. Chester arrived in a smart new suit bought for the occasion and bearing the silver knife, fork and spoon considered appropriate. He enjoyed the christening, where he read 'Wystan's lines' and was properly serious, although when it came to renouncing 'the devil and all his works' he couldn't resist adding under his breath, 'collected'. The ceremony at St James' American church was short, but the party that followed at our house in Via Ugo Foscolo was festive; more spumante than champagne, but festive nonetheless. Among the guests was a young American couple, bright and attractive but exhaustingly *au courant*. They dressed in the latest fashion, read the latest books, played the latest music, and danced the latest dances. Talking politics with them was like reading the next day's newspapers, and conversation was filled with tomorrow's phrases. We called them 'the groovies' as that was their latest word for the latest pleasure when we first met. They brought Simon a lovely christening mug, and with it they also brought a large white paper scroll, decorated with flowers, on which they had written 'Welcome to the race, baby. Be Kind.' Chester objected to the lack of skill in the presentation (the flowers were crudely drawn, the lettering sloppy); John objected to the message; I was so filled with well-being that I merely smiled and said, 'Wait till we tell Wystan.' That evening Wystan rang up to see how things had gone. I think he wanted a report on Chester in church. Wystan used the telephone sparingly and awkwardly – more grunts, mumbles and silences than conversation, as though he wanted to hide something from the machine. We all had a word with him, brief in the interests of economy, and when I told him about the groovies' scroll he became more incoherent than usual. The thought of kindness being the ultimate virtue upset him as much as the language.

By the time the last guest had left and the waiters hired for the occasion had cleared up, Simon was ready for his ten o'clock feed. I brought him outside to the *aia* and John, Chester and I settled down to finish the left-over canapés and spumante and to discuss the day. It was warm, soothingly so, and the rhyncospermum climbing up the front of the house was in full flower. Simon and I must have dropped off to sleep together, as the conversation seemed to come and go. I awoke to a gentle laugh from both men, and shifted Simon to the other breast. Chester had written in his head a poem for the christening. I found it moving and begged him to write it down; he never did. All I can remember is a line that, after a series of wishes for Simon's future, went 'May what is, be what should be.'

During that visit Chester asked John and me to go with him on a trip to Cattolica, a fishing village on the Adriatic coast. Alessandro had married and moved there, and Chester wanted to see him 'just once more'. We set out (fairly) early on a Sunday morning, but stopped for lunch and didn't arrive at Alessandro's house until almost three, to be told he had gone to the Circolo to play cards. When we got there – a Communist-run recreation centre – Chester's nerve failed him and he asked John to go in and bring Alessandro out to the car. John, whose Italian is perfect though strongly Tuscan, went in and introduced himself to a suspicious Alessandro saying, 'I'm John Clark.' Alessandro growled, '*E con questo?*' – meaning more or less 'So what?' 'I'm a friend of Chester Kallman,' said John. 'MADONNA!' said Alessandro. In the car there were handshakes all round and a certain amount of forced laughter. We went back to the house – a square, newish box with a neat vegetable garden and two terracotta dogs guarding the entrance – and were presented to his pregnant wife and two-year-old son. We had coffee sitting around the table in a spotless kitchen. The sturdy two-year-old was the centre of attention until the praise, genuine though it was, became too much for him and he hid behind his mother's chair. John told an amusing story about Simon's birth, and Chester described our lunch in detail. The half-hour or so passed quickly. Alessandro took us out to the car and we all embraced. As we drove away Chester said, 'He deserves a beautiful baby,' and burst into tears.

Simon was born on May 28th, 1965, so he was not quite three months old when we took him for the first time to Kirchstetten. He was a normal healthy baby who slept, ate and occasionally acknowledged an admirer. John and I were besotted with him, but I worried that others might not be so enchanted – especially if he disturbed the zealously protected routine. There was no problem: he was welcomed, examined and pronounced a success. Frau Ei looked him over carefully – with her hands clasped behind her back – and asked John if she might take him to her house. She picked up the carrying basket, never touching the baby, and took him to see the pond and meet her cats. Chester sang to him, unsuitable songs, and Wystan imitated his gurgles. Simon and Wystan sensed when each had had enough of the other: attention was intense but brief. After the first night, I began – at Wystan's suggestion – to give Simon his last evening feed at table, between nine and ten o'clock. Nursing Simon at the table became so much a part of our day that Chester felt cheated and Wystan offended on the one night that Simon overslept. That year a great deal of conversation centred on the laws of nature, the difference between 'ought' and 'must'.

The 'dear little poem', as Chester called it, that he had been working on in our garden was finally finished. He showed it to Wystan in our presence that summer. Wystan said, cautiously, I thought: 'Very beautiful, my dear, and very original, though I'm not quite sure what it is all about, except by a kind of osmosis; in spots that is.' Chester wasn't at all offended: as a matter of fact we joked about it, as neither John nor I could figure it out either. It seemed obscure, almost hopelessly so, but it *'suonava bene'* as the Italians say (meaning, the sounds are pleasant, even hypnotic, rather like Poe or Mallarmé), and that seemed to be enough for Chester at the moment. He said he would put it away, leaving it in a warm spot so that it would 'ripen like Liederkranz and become immediately perceptible to the public'. By 'public' he meant *his* public, and we all spent a while defining that. It seemed strange that Chester was so unemotional about something he cared for so deeply. It seemed even stranger a few nights later. Chester had made an elaborate Bavarian Cream for Lisa and two young friends. We 'grown-ups' seldom ate sweets. He bore a magnificent rosy mound to the table in triumph, only to have it collapse before our eyes. He burst into tears and ran from the room. The collapse of both Chester and the pudding was so complete that the rest of us could only sit and sigh. Not a snigger, even from the young. 'There must,' said Wystan, 'be something wrong with the recipe.'

On the last day of January 1968 John and I moved from Via Ugo Foscolo to the house in the country south of Florence where we still live. Our first important social event was Anita Auden's wedding in May. Anita was John and Sheila's elder daughter and, like her mother, a beauty. We managed to do away with naked lightbulbs and dry out our dining room (it had been the stable and the animals' breath had permeated the walls) just in time. The groom's parents had a villa in Florence and as his mother was ill it was decided to celebrate the wedding here. Anita, Wystan and Chester stayed with us and John and Sheila at a nearby hotel. The reception was held at our house. Both Wystan and Chester were enthusiastic and plans were made and remade. Wystan believed in marriage: 'Any marriage,' he said, 'happy or unhappy, is more interesting than a love affair.' He made a tremendous effort to come to the wedding as on April 23rd he had broken his shoulder in an accident. A letter from Chester told us that on his way home from shopping 'Wystan, trying to save a bag of eggs from slipping fatally off the front seat of the car, bent over to reach down with his right hand, balanced (brilliantly) by raising his (on the wheel) left hand, and swerved directly into a telegraph pole.' The comments in brackets are Chester's, not mine. Chester continued, 'Result: a fractured right shoulder which (until May 8th) is encased and propped up in a Rococo "device" that holds his arm in perpetual half-salute, weighs him into eternal fatigue, and is very convenient for carving runnels on coffee tables. In any case, he can't write, so I, who also can't write (for myself) am now doing so for him.' This to announce their arrival in time for the wedding.

At any rate on May 10th Wystan and Chester made the sixteen-hour train journey to Florence. Wystan told us that when he saw the telegraph pole approaching he said, 'No, no! He couldn't, not to His ewe lamb!' He could: it was a multiple fracture.

Anita was a lovely bride. Her slightly Audenesque features (to me she looked very much like a photograph of her Auden grandmother) were softened by her mother's beauty. When John Auden was working in India he fell in love with and married a woman whose dazzling looks matched her impeccable Brahmin antecedents. Anita's skin was golden, her eyes inky black. There was a simple traditional service in St Mark's

English church where Wystan bellowed out the responses, Chester looked embarrassed and Simon was a reluctant page. Simon's language was Italian, his English was limited to the phrase 'How-u-do-vere-wel-tank-u', which he used for his responses. I was cross with Wystan and John. They had taken Simon, aged three, to have his hair trimmed, but had got into a discussion of the antithesis between holy and unholy joy and didn't notice the barber cutting off all of Simon's long blond hair. They were apologetic and Simon was delighted.

I slipped out of the church as soon as decently possible to get home to oversee the reception. The guests were the groom's family, plus old friends of ours and Wystan's, a few young and a few very young. The groom was tall and pleasant and rich, with the crinkly blond hair that some Englishmen have. None of Chester's special friends could make the wedding; he apologized for their absence. A pair of Chester's burly bricklayers might have added a certain colour, but I felt we had confused the groom's family enough as it was. The British Consul, Harold Acton, a titled Italian couple who spoke English, and a younger son of a British ducal family, made up to the groom's family for the Indian blood that was coming their way.

There was a warm reunion between Wystan and Harold, who hadn't seen each other in years. Harold had been in his last year at Christ Church when Wystan went up to Oxford; that kind of glamour lasts a lifetime. Sheila looked cloudless, beautiful and very Brahmin, and John Auden was at his most charming. All went smoothly, although the groom's father was heard to ask the Consul if the eccentric-looking man, the bride's uncle, really was well known. The wedding photographs show a delighted Wystan. He and Sheila alone seem unaware of the photographer. For those who, like me, want to know how happy endings end, there was a divorce but there was also an exceptional son.

After the reception was over, Wystan, Chester, John and I went to a local trattoria and talked and talked. About the wedding Wystan said that marriage seemed to him to require three important things: patience, foresight and manoeuvre. 'Like war,' said Chester. We talked about Thomas Hardy. We argued about his heroines – Chester and I against the others. We were filled with admiration for women ruled by their passions; for John, Hardy heroines were conceived to illustrate the author's ideas, and Wystan maintained that they displayed the proper balance between self-confidence and humility. Voices were raised as each tried to put his point across. John turned his argument into a theory and Chester turned his into a performance. Wystan said that he and I were the only 'true intuitives', the difference being that he was 'thinking intuitive'. By then everyone had offended everyone else. We were all appeased when Wystan said, 'We should all be grateful to Hardy; I most of all.' So we ordered another *fiasco* of Chianti and changed the subject. Late in the evening, all of us quite drunk, Wystan said, 'I might have enjoyed being John' (meaning his brother). 'Who would have been Wystan, then?' I asked. We were all too tired and crocked to pursue this, fortunately.

Within John Auden's family Chester had a substantial role which he seemed to enjoy. He had enchanted Sheila and the girls, and John was fond of him as well. John was angry with what he considered unfair criticism of Chester in the press. A letter in February 1970 says: 'There is a revolting article on Wystan (and even unkinder on Chester) in the February number of *Harpers*. Much of what Wystan is reported as saying certainly rings true, but with twists. Chester is made to appear a buffoon . . . "a gross ungainly man with dull and knobbly eyes, he has the look of one too old to play the naughty cherub anymore". Some people seem out to make mischief and to wound behind a screen of slick and vulgar reporting.' I wondered how many attacks of this kind Chester learned about. He knew he was being criticized, being judged both for himself and for what some considered his effect on

Wystan, but no matter how battered his ego was it was a strong one. And he managed to endure or ignore most criticism, even the most malevolent. Wystan as a well-known man received praise and admiration but also engendered envy and disapproval. Chester became an easy target both for Wystan's friends and for his enemies. Some blamed Chester for everything in Wystan that disappointed them. Some blamed America.

My lasting image of John Auden is the solitary figure pacing up and down in front of the room in Kirchstetten where Wystan's coffin lay. Wystan hadn't been an easy brother but the attachment was deep. If there was jealousy between them it was from Wystan's side. John was a scientist and a father, two things Wystan yearned to be. The eldest brother, Bernard, had a minor role, although both John and Wystan admired his children. Once I mentioned to John Auden how upset Wystan had been when a letter from his mother reached him after her death. John told me that it had happened to him, too. He had such a weary look that I understood having Wystan as a younger brother had its difficult moments. Wystan wrote a letter of protest to *The Times* when their father's obituary was published and there was scarcely any mention of John, who had conducted the first Geological Survey of India and was one of the foremost geologists in the world. The letter was never published.

We had seen a great deal of John and Sheila during a family crisis in 1963. Anita, then just down from Oxford, had come to Florence to live with us and help Lisa with her English. Lisa, aged twelve, had always gone to Italian or German schools and although she spoke English without an accent we caught her reading *Olivero Twist*. The idea of Dickens in Italian convinced us that she should go to England for further schooling. Anita came to stay for several months to prepare her for entrance exams. Lisa adored Anita and was soon reading proper Dickens and writing Gothic tales. It was an extremely satisfactory arrangement until Anita came down with a mysterious and violent illness. What had seemed to be bronchitis turned ugly, her fever soared and her body became covered with purple bruises. Our doctor rushed over at six in the morning and immediately ordered an ambulance; he feared, correctly, a virulent form of meningitis. This happened on Good Friday, and Anita was not out of danger until the following Wednesday. Her convalescence was long and tedious. John and Sheila flew to Milan and took a taxi to Florence, arriving early on Easter morning. Sheila sat wordlessly by Anita's bed, stroking her arm. John paced up and down in the corridor muttering 'intolerable'. Wystan sent a telegram saying he 'knew' it was going to end well and Chester accused us of having germs lurking in our cupboards. John and Sheila stayed with us in Via Ugo Foscolo during the weeks of Anita's convalescence, and we spent a great deal of time in late-night conversations, since we were all talkers. One night, filled with Christian arrogance and too much wine, I made the mistake of asking Sheila when she had converted. 'Oh, my dear, I never converted,' she said. 'You see we Hindus believe that everyone has the religion he is mature enough for.' How that statement related to Wystan's Anglicanism and her husband's Catholicism I never quite found out. Sheila was amused by the Europeans who traced their ancestors to the Renaissance or to the Middle Ages. 'You see,' she said, 'we go back to mythology; our ancestors we trace to the Sun and the Moon.' John said that Wystan's accounts of their childhood were accurate, as far as they went; he, too, had sung duets with their mother. Sheila talked a great deal about Chester's charm.

Wystan often stayed with us *en route* from New York to Austria, after a stop-over in London. I particularly remember one visit of two weeks during the Easter vacation of 1971. Lisa and two young friends drove with me to collect him at the airport in Pisa. He arrived around noon on a sunlit day in early April – the 2nd, I think. He had had a good flight, sitting next to an English maritime historian. Wystan liked to pass himself off to strangers as a medieval historian so they had begun a conversation as colleagues. It was not until the professor became technical and boring that Wystan said he was jealous of anyone who was 'paid for studying sailors'. Wystan told us the story as we were waiting for his bags, and pointed out a bewildered man in tweeds. Wystan was oblivious to the strain of travel. New surroundings always stimulated him, either to immediate anger or delight.

On the back road from Pisa to Lucca is a hill covered with well-tended olive trees; from it one can see Pisa's Campo dei Miracoli on the distant plain. We picnicked there after scrambling up the side of the hill. The young were surprised at Wystan's agility and remarked on it in what seemed to me condescending tones. He was delighted at their praise. Lisa, remembering Kirchstetten, found a large flat stone for Wystan to sit on, and although he disliked cold food ('It makes one think that mother didn't care') he enjoyed the picnic as much as the rest of us. One of the boys was reading English at Oxford and had just discovered the Scots poet Dunbar, whose lines both he and Wystan recited. All that strange, lovely language went to my head, together with the wine. The ground had lost its winter chill, the light was full of promise, and the beaten-silver leaves of the olive trees gave a classical touch to the scene. It was a proper feast, satiety for all the senses.

Afterwards we went to the Pieve of San Piero in Grado, side-stepping the restoration work and straining to see those fascinating early frescos. By the time we reached home we were all exhausted from a day in which everything was funny or beautiful or both. Wystan maintained that laughter was not the proper way to express joy – it should be song. That day laughter was sufficient. We played the translation game, with Wystan, as one would expect, the winner. I can't remember many of the gems but I do remember all of us having hysterics at *elettrodomestici* as robots and the *Trovatore* aria '*Il balen del suo sorriso'* as 'What a whale of a smile'. The object of the game is to take one or more words that sound alike but can be interpreted quite differently and change their meaning completely. It was a heady, Tuscan spring day that I, for one, will never forget.

When visiting, Wystan always kept to a strict routine. Mornings, after coffee, cigarettes and the crossword, he worked in John's study. He closed the door and all the shutters and worked by the light of a single table lamp whose 100 watt bulb pleased him. He was silent, but somehow his presence was felt throughout the house.

In those days we had a couple working for us, Bruno and Bruna, known as *I Bruni* or 'The Browns'. They had worked on the land of the Principe Cenci, whose huge villa overlooked our house. There they had learned that mixture of deference and familiarity that was fast disappearing. It was *paternalismo*, but it was they who were paternal to us; the arrangement worked admirably. They both took to Wystan; Bruna enjoyed sprucing him up (his frayed shirt cuffs were a challenge), and Bruno, who was religious, would ask doctrinal questions, which Wystan answered willingly. At first *I Bruni* addressed Wystan as *'eccellenza'*, until I persuaded them that was too formal. Then it was 'Don Ugo' as they couldn't manage any form of Wystan or Auden and were pleased to learn that 'Hugh' translated. The 'Don' was priestly.

After working all morning, Wystan came down for Campari (dubbed 'Campy soda' by Chester) promptly at 12.30, followed by lunch at one. Afternoons were for sightseeing or drives in the country or visiting. Evenings were for long, wine-filled dinners. Lisa was home for the Easter vacation and was usually accompanied by friends, so there was always a tableful. Wystan loved it. He particularly liked something he called, 'shocking the young'. He was so adept at this that one night the boy we called 'little Tony' had to go out for a walk before the fruit.

Dinner-table conversations had no limit either to subject or to opinion. Wystan was far more tolerant than I about the ideas of the young; I was often tempted to pooh-pooh and to change the subject. Wystan said that although their beliefs were sometimes foolish they were never false, and that he felt the young (at least these young) genuinely wanted each other to be better. 'Have you noticed,' he asked, 'the intense interest and attention that they pay to each other's ideas?' I hadn't, but from then on I did.

In Ischia we had all enjoyed the celebrations for local feast days. Here in the sophisticated centre of the country few of the traditions remained. One that does, however, is the Blessing of the House, before Easter. All over Florence on the days up to Holy Week priests in freshly ironed surplices, accompanied by one or two acolytes, censers swinging, go about their business, dispensing God's blessing. They also bring good fortune, chase away evil spirits and check on the ritual spring cleaning.

Our priest in the country travels by Fiat, having graduated from an old Vespa. He blesses every room in the house, unless the house is too large or last year's tip was too small. One day I came home from shopping to find the acolytes playing with Simon's toys and Wystan deep in conversation with Don Mario. Wystan was explaining to him, in heavily accented but correct Italian, that liturgy, as the bridge from the unborn to the dead, should be performed in a language that need not, in fact, should not, be understood. Don Mario was young and full of reform; he probably still remembered everything he had learned in the seminary. On his face was a look of great concern, although I certainly couldn't tell if the worry was for himself or for Wystan. He sprang to his feet, gathered his acolytes around him like a protective garment, and rushed out of the house hardly waiting for his tip. Wystan never altered his conversation or his ideas for his audience. He would use the same theological argument with Reinhold Niebuhr that he used with our local country priest. I never saw Wystan in pursuit, but when I asked Chester if he changed his approach even then, Chester only giggled, so I never found out.

I think it was during that same Easter vacation that Wystan and I (John was working) went to visit friends in the Chianti. They were a young couple, Maro and Matthew Spender. Matthew was the son of Wystan's great friends Stephen and Natasha. Some coolness had developed between the Spender generations, and Wystan had promised he would do his best to ease the situation. I was less than enthusiastic when he announced his intentions, since tact was not one of Wystan's major gifts. We accepted an invitation to lunch, and drove the hour and a bit to their house in the middle of a thunderstorm. Wystan delighted in the intensity of the storm and the winding country road (none of that Roman arrogance of cutting through the countryside). We never stopped talking all the way out. At one moment I noticed that Wystan looked uncomfortable, almost green. We were in the middle of a theory of his that without human individuality there can be no humour, but he accepted my offer to stop the car. 'Wise, I think,' he said, and he got out and was violently sick at the side of the road. Getting back into the car he said, '. . . that is why primitives have no real sense of humour.'

As we neared the house he practised what he would say to the young husband. The situation bothered him. When we arrived and I saw the trouble that had been taken, I hoped he would use the second of his practised approaches, the avuncular as opposed to the firm, dictatorial one. As a matter of fact what he actually did was turn to Matthew and say, 'Your father loves you very much, you know.' On the way home I questioned him about his role as messenger and he replied, 'It seemed to be the only thing worth saying.' I couldn't have agreed more.

I never understood all those complaints about Wystan as a house guest. We found him relaxed and not at all demanding, but then meals were always on time at our house. He was punctilious about thank-you letters. A typical one reads: 'I don't need to tell you that I had a wonderful time with you both. It was *lovely*. Thanks ever so: Love to the dogs and cat and lots to you both.' This was from Berlin on February 25th, 1965, after the birthday he spent with us. Our household suited him in other ways too. We live in an old and rather battered house in the middle of the Tuscan countryside, and although seen from a distance the house looks grand, up close the effect is very different. It is really a strange jumble of rooms built around an ancient stone watch-tower. For generations it was used as a farmhouse for huge patriarchal families, and each family built on a room when needed. The result is confusing, but does give a considerable amount of privacy. The handsomest part of the house is the tower, which is divided into four floors. The room at the very top was the one that Wystan chose as his. The stairs leading to the top-tower were little more than a wooden ladder, but it never seemed to bother him. He never, as a matter of principle, went to his room during the day, so he had to negotiate the steps only once up and once down each day. He boasted about his agility so much that one night we all assembled, at his request, to watch the performance of his ascent.

These visits reinforced my belief about Wystan's need for 'home'. He was delighted to go out, to a party, to sightsee or just for a drive but he was always the first to ask to 'go home', even when he was obviously enjoying himself. Was he worried about wasting time, I asked once. He assured me that nothing was wasted, so it must have been the need to return. At his fifty-eighth birthday party in Via Ugo Foscolo he said, as he and I were drunkenly sitting on the edge of the bathtub trying to escape the festivities downstairs, and have a moment alone: 'I'm not ready to go home yet.' It was said with such a mixture of determination and longing that it sobered us both up, temporarily.

Near our house was a stone barn that had long been unused. Wystan asked, rather timidly I thought, if we had any plans for renovating it, as he thought it would make an ideal place for him to spend his winters. John began enthusiastically drawing up plans. To this day I regret my behaviour; I was lukewarm.

For several years I had been aware that life in New York, where they spent the winter months, was not going well for either of them. A letter from a concerned friend said (it was undated but a second paragraph went on to say that JFK had just made his announcement about the Cuban missile crisis): 'I am trying not to get *too* offended by W and C. I underline the "too" advisedly because, to tell the truth, it's hard not to get offended by them recently. I can't figure out what has gotten into them, but it seems to be some sort of pattern now after a year or two. I go through a yearly winter neurosis – to call or not to call, to care or not to care. Do they care? If not, why not? It's not Chester so much, since he is usually very friendly and glad to see me, but of course he's also lazy as hell and never calls or writes anybody. And Wystan is, I don't know how to describe it, but sort of crabby (at least, in desperation that's what last spring just before he left I told him he was – and he said that he was amazed that I could ever possibly imagine that he was crabby!), but I also asked Chester at one point if Wystan was getting crabby and he said emphatically YES and not just to me but to everybody. WHY, who knows? I suspect he is sort of sick of people in general, all people except when he feels particularly lonesome, but with his strength of character that doesn't happen too often. I hate to say it but I dread knowing that they are going to be in town because it will start all over again. I suppose one can live without them, but one would like to make sure first that one decides that because really and truly they can live without one.'

This was from someone whose friendship Wystan and Chester valued a great deal. I thought about it and wondered if the state of the world was not partly responsible for Wystan's fits of ill humour (none of which *we* had seen). He had made some bitter remarks about the stupidity of world

79

leaders, and was expounding the doctrine that the world should be run by women and Swedish bureaucrats – until he actually went to Sweden, that is. I began to believe that in New York he felt both too involved, and too helpless. He longed for calm judgement, wisdom and humour, none of which he found there.

Wystan's letters from New York seemed to me to be filled with disappointment. 'Naughty Chester has, of course, not written nor, which is more serious, sent me any lyrics for the *Don Quixote* musical, the producer-director of which is breathing down my neck. Cooking is rather a problem, especially because my doctor has put me on a diet – no butter, no salt, and I may only roast or boil. However, I manage. On Monday next I have to go to Yale for ten days and be nice to students. The heart sinks.' The *Don Quixote* musical mentioned here turned out to be *Man of La Mancha*, which made its actual authors rich.

One of the reasons we got on so well with Wystan was the ease . . . I had a feeling that the tensions in their relationship dissolved in the general laughter. Chester could chat up anybody. It wasn't just the jokes and the performances that Wystan admired, it was the ease. We were among the very few people they saw a great deal of who were neither musical/ literary or sexual friends. Wystan said again and again that there was one thing the people he really loved had in common; they all made him laugh; to me a proper yardstick. What made us laugh? Almost everything some evenings, and it wasn't just the wine; it was contagious. The laughter passed from one to another like a gift. There is something wonderfully isolating about laughter; it makes everything else stop. I find myself smiling even now at the thought of the laughter. Each laughed in a very different fashion. John began laughing long before anyone got to the point; Chester tried to keep it back until the proper moment but often couldn't manage, and exploded like a bursting faucet; Wystan threw his head back and roared, although he was always the first to stop. Once, weak from laughter at some performance of Chester's, I couldn't help saying how lovely it was and how much 'better' I felt myself to be when I was happy. 'Nonsense,' said Wystan disapprovingly. 'Happiness isn't a moral force, it's a duty.' As he said in 'The Poet and The City': '. . . among the half dozen or so things for which a man of honour should be prepared, if necessary, to die, the right to play, the right to frivolity, is not the least.'

Wystan often had what I called, for want of a better word, 'crushes' on women. There was no sexual involvement, but the desire was there. Unlike Chester, who sought comfort and warmth in his female friends, Wystan liked to admire, even covet. When we first met he talked a great deal about Ursula Niebuhr and how wonderful it would be to be married to 'the most brilliant woman theologian alive'. There was a long-standing affinity with Nancy Spender, the widow of Michael, Stephen's younger brother killed in the war, whom he loved for her spirit and her adventures. There was the widow of a fellow poet, whom he admired for her beauty and her understanding of his work. When he discovered her opinions were those of her late husband recited by rote, the romance cooled. In the later years there was a warm friendship with a handsome Englishwoman married to a local Graf living near Kirchstetten. These attachments, and there were others like them, meant a great deal to Wystan. Chester made fun of the women and the attachments, but he was jealous. Wystan, as opposed to Chester, found himself strongly attracted to women. His attachment to his niece Rita was an example; although he loved both of John's daughters, he at one time had a real 'crush' on Rita. He carried a photograph of her around with him and showed me a series of drawings representing the five senses in which he claimed to see a strong resemblance. She reminded him of his mother, and he managed to bring her name into the conversation often; he praised her strength of character and was pleased and proud of her success. 'Rita has passed her F.R.C.S. primary exam, and operates in 2 hospitals, as well as doing research on prostatic dogs,' he wrote. 'She seems to be specializing in the lower orifices.'

Not that Wystan was uncritical of those he loved, it was only that he preferred to praise. He refused to review a book he didn't like. 'It is too easy to be clever,' he said, 'when the material is inferior, as well as a waste of time.'

Wystan talked a great deal about money, and he wrote about it, too. A family joke, often repeated and as boring as these things usually are, was his resemblance to his father in their stinginess about the use of loo paper. Once Sheila arrived in Kirchstetten bearing rolls and rolls of violet-tinted perfumed paper to tease him out of his fixation. He was delighted, and immediately invited her back for the following year.

Money as a reward for work had little meaning for him. He once showed me a substantial cheque, payment for an article that had taken him two hours to write. A poem that had taken agonies had brought him only a fraction of that sum. Bills had to be paid and Wystan took a certain satisfaction in his ability to earn a living; his poetry he wrote for love.

In all his life Wystan never possessed any significant sum of money, but he was generous with what he had. Money channelled through Father Lustkandle had paid for the education of several promising local young. One summer when we were visiting we met two of the beneficiaries. These particular young men had done well in their exams and had come to be congratulated by their sponsor. Wystan was nervous and slightly abashed; he thought these things should be done anonymously, but the good Father had insisted on the meeting. There was a considerable bustle preparing tea and cakes, and a search, in vain, for six matching cups. Two scrubbed youths arrived, carefully dressed in freshly ironed shirts and sharply creased trousers. The conversation was, of course, in German, with a few stilted phrases in English for me. Any note of gratitude was quickly and neatly circumvented. One lad played the cello and the other was a mountain-climber, and, after due praise for the cakes, the talk scarcely strayed from these subjects. Two smiling lads left after the proper forty-five minutes and the visit was pronounced a success. The next summer I asked about the boys and Wystan indicated that the chapter was closed since the boys were now self-sufficient.

When Wystan talked to Chester about household expenses, we felt he wasn't talking about money as such. Wystan was actually, John said, talking about economy, the economy necessary in an established solid 'household'. A friend suggested that things might have gone better for the two of them had Chester been able to earn a living. Perhaps. Wystan, as patriarch, wanted to push Chester out into the world, wanted a recognition of Chester's considerable talents. He was anything but subtle in this. He almost destroyed an important friendship for Chester by continually saying, 'Why can't you be more like Bill Weaver?'

When our son Simon was five, during The Visit of 1970, Chester took me aside to have a serious talk. He and Wystan had been discussing what they considered a problem and thought I should be told about it. The problem turned out to be Simon's excessive charm. 'Dangerous,' said Wystan. 'Could be fatal,' said Chester. 'He's only five,' said I. They both felt it was too easy to become dependent on charm, especially for a male child raised in a Latin country. 'But I love it!' I said, and then felt a fool as I saw their knowing looks. 'Quite acceptable for a political hostess or a minor diplomat,' said Wystan; 'Surely he'll do better than that,' said Chester. They had given the matter a great deal of thought. They had reached the same conclusion but I felt that they had arrived by very different paths. Wystan (who knew himself to be an addictive type) was worried that the habit could develop and be difficult to eradicate later, so that all of his 'works are but / Extensions of his power to Charm'. Chester was himself suffering from an overdependence on charm and tried in his way to warn me.

Wystan knew what he wanted: for himself, from himself and from others. He was well aware that there would be gaps, unbridgeable distances between fulfilment and desire, but he did not pretend to fill the voids. Chester only wished; he actually thought his wishes could and would come true. I remember once, well into the last years, he told me a story. In Athens he caught a visitor going through his pockets. When challenged the boy said he thought of Chester as his father and that certainly could not be considered stealing. Chester was moved by the boy's story and I had sense enough to keep quiet.

Compare this with what happened to Wystan when he found his Austrian boyfriend had been sent to jail for stealing. The young man, whose name was Hugerl, was a pick-up from Vienna. When Wystan was away in New York, he had used the Volkswagen for a series of robberies, one of which was from the house in Kirchstetten. Wystan, after persuasion from Chester, felt it his duty to help him, saying the boy had a fifty per cent chance of leading a decent life when he got out of prison, since he had paid his debt. He paid for Hugie, as he was known, to go to a vocational school. When Hugie became a specialist master-mechanic, a title that sounds grander in German, Wystan was pleased. As he said in a poem, 'both learned a lesson'. The relationship continued after Hugie's marriage, and cocktails with the wife became a part of Wystan's Fridays.

Wishes seem to me to be self-destructive. Not the childish ones for long golden curls and a perfect singing voice, but the wishes divorced from true or false or good or evil that Chester indulged in. Chester never tried to use other people to gain his own ends, but he was so utterly self-obsessed that he conceived of the world only through his own fantasy and wishes.

His world was as subjective as that of a small child. I remember once in Florence when we had a table full of holiday guests and Chester said to me, 'How lovely he (I forget his name) is by candlelight.' This for an overweight, under-washed pick-up in a clinging white dacron polo-shirt, when everyone else at the table was young, dressed in his best and animated. That he saw his lovers only through his personal wishes for them meant that they scarcely existed outside of his imagination. Interestingly, to me, he sought explanations for his lovers' faults in his own behaviour. (When one of them stole from the house, it was because Chester had spoken to him harshly.) He never claimed responsibility for their virtues, only their faults. He was strangely selfless in spite of his enormously strong persona. As he grew older he needed more and more fantasies to explain, to justify himself, and to bury his despondency.

Chester had had a miserable childhood. He was convinced that his mother's death from a blood clot was the result of an illegal abortion forced on her by his father. Whether this had any basis in truth, I have no idea, but he believed it unquestioningly.

Once he told me about his father's second wife, the mother of his half-brother. His half-brother as a child wrote a poem called 'My Brother', that went, 'I have a brother / and my mother / hates my brother.' It was then, during the reign of the wicked stepmother, that he taught himself how to be happy. He would go alone to the seaside, wish himself far away, and dream. Two constants in Chester's life were the sea and dreams. 'Missing the Sea' is to me one of the best poems he ever wrote and was his own personal favourite.

One dreadful story sticks in my mind; a story first told me by an old friend and then by Chester himself. The wording in both versions was identical. Chester won a scholarship for graduate work at the University of Michigan and asked his father to lend him the money for the train fare to Ann Arbor. His father refused him, saying, 'You know how to get it yourself' – which, of course, he did. It was hardly surprising that Chester could never accept the person he actually was but needed wishes and fantasies to soften the self-despair.

There was in Chester's mind a great desire for logic and a certain kind of order. He loved all manner of problems, cryptograms, puzzles and the like, even ones as simple as the crosswords at which he excelled, and he delighted in working out an opera libretto so that each syllable could be properly sung. He whose life was so chaotic had a compelling need for discipline and order in his work; as though his inner life was an antidote to his behaviour. I have always found Chester's poetry difficult. It is often too intricate for me, as if he had devised a tantalizing riddle that I am not bright enough to solve. Wystan, on the other hand, seemed to go out of his way to make his work understandable, even easy. How often I have read a line of Wystan's and thought, 'Why, of course, I knew *that!*' Once, in my cups, I thanked him for writing so directly for me, and I think he was pleased.

Chester as a theatrical thinker as well as a performer felt the need for a finale, something that would bring down the curtain. When he finished a scene he at once rushed on to the next problem. Wystan was not wrong when he pronounced Chester 'far cleverer and quicker than I am'. His mind worked too quickly. This showed even in his cooking. A dinner might consist of a spectacular dish such as a perfectly boned, pressed duck prepared with a skill that few professionals could match, but followed by nothing else; he never served coffee or bread of any kind. It didn't matter to us, as what he did serve was so delicious, but a serious chef would have been appalled. He concentrated on the spectacular and forgot or didn't care about the rest. Planning meals was a pleasure for him and he loved to talk about it. The kitchen was filled with cookbooks, and he made it a point of honour to try at least one recipe from each, the most difficult one, of course. He would meet us when we arrived with 'Norwegian Fish Pie, never tried

86

before', or some other equally tempting offer. People didn't worry about cholesterol in those days, and it was just as well, as many of Chester's recipes were of the 'take two pints of heavy cream, one pound of butter, twelve eggs' variety.

Dinner to Chester was always a performance – a solo aria – in which he took pride. Dinner to Wystan was the high point in the day's routine. He made a great to-do, rushing around closing the curtains, setting up the plate-warmer and checking the place settings at table. I sometimes felt that the pleasure he took in these tasks was not the prospect of the evening's relaxation so much as a thankfulness that the day was over. As he grew older, he, too, put on weight. It must have been from drink and lack of exercise for he ate less and less as he aged, although he always welcomed Chester's experiments in the kitchen. Chester used his cooking as an excuse as well as a justification: a letter could not be answered or the soufflé would fall; a translation was unfinished but the Cumberland sauce was perfect. Once when Wystan was thundery about some minor transgression I saw Chester retreat to stir the soup five times during the conversation. On another occasion, Chester wrote: 'Oh yes. Wystan is terribly upset that he hasn't heard from Neil about the Goethe. I made the dreadful tactful error, when I returned from Italy, of assuring him that the book had been sent. Last night I confessed all. He was furious. I fled into the kitchen until the clouds passed. Kitchens are a great invention.' Chester had promised to send Neil a copy of *Italian Journey*, had forgotten and then told Wystan he had done so – another minor transgression exacerbated by a foolish fib. I wrote to Chester asking just what a 'tactful' error was. He never answered.

I asked friends in New York what Chester's father had been like. 'Jovial,' they said. He was, I was told, 'a theatrical raconteur and a good cook. People sort of liked him,' said my friend, although admitting that his jokes were not very clever and his 'sensibility' was coarse. A more concerned friend said, 'He always put Chester down in public.' How could Chester, who agonized over slights and offences, real or imaginary, ever have forgiven his father? His desire for his father's approval must have been greater and stronger than any of us could have imagined. In 1971 he dedicated a volume of poetry, *The Sense of Occasion*, to his father and his mistress (who in Chester-speak was known as Miss Mistress). His first volume of poetry he dedicated to Wystan, the second to James Schuyler. I never met either Chester's father or his mistress, whom he married at Chester's death. Some friends say that Dorothy (the wife) was in love with Chester and only took his father as second-best. She has been described as tall, slim and ethereal, floating along with a scarf trailing, à la Isadora. They say she was especially ethereal when drunk. When she stopped drinking she became even more ethereal and some-what spiritual, to look at, that is. Wystan deeply disliked Chester's father, whom he blamed for Chester's miserable childhood, but he was polite. The father and his wife were invited to large parties, and Chester at one time spent quite a bit of time with them. Chester never said a word against Dorothy and when in New York spoke to her on the telephone almost daily. Once he sent Dorothy a dress from Greece as a birthday present. He wrote to me, 'I heard from Pete Butorac that the dress arrived safely in New York. Mad Dorothy said that it was a miraculous gift and she couldn't imagine who sent it. It took quite a little prodding from Pete to make her connect the Kallman on the return address with me. REALLY.' They inherited everything at Chester's death, including all of Wystan's copyrights.

Pride – I don't mean the deadly sin against God – I mean the ordinary personal pride more properly called vanity – is an obstacle in any relationship. With Wystan and Chester it was a disaster. While at one time or another each was prepared to humble himself, to make amends, it seemed to me that neither was ever prepared to accept the other's sacrifice, or even to acknowledge it as such. Nor could they recognize each other's vulnerability. Each thought the other could take it, and sometimes they went too far. It became obvious that neither could or would 'win' as neither would give in or give up.

Why did Chester fight Wystan so – a fight that brought both such unhappiness? (Had it begun, I wondered, with an unconscious wish to bind Wystan to him, never to let him forget just who was causing the suffering?) John, who was his confidant in those last years, says the struggle had by then assumed terrifying proportions in Chester's mind. Losing had become a completely irrational fear, rather like a primitive who believes a photograph will take away his spirit. Perhaps he was aware of those critics who felt that he, as the lesser talent, should sacrifice himself to the greater. Wystan wanted and needed him; some people thought that should be enough for Chester. There are wives or companions who are satisfied to be the power behind the throne: not Chester. He was furious, and hurt, when a highly respectable lady poet said, 'What a shame Chester doesn't write a cookbook.' This remark was relayed to him the day after it was made.

Withholding part of himself from Wystan became a necessity. I believe that Wystan felt this and accepted Chester's needs, no matter how much personal misery they caused him, just as he had accepted responsibility for Chester's life. In the early years Chester would say things like 'writing in Wystan's shadow', which seemed a harmless enough remark, unless a soothing shade turned deep and dark enough to blot out the light. As a matter of fact they were happiest when they were collaborating. Chester felt the partnership was equal, or nearly so, and Wystan, who had no self-doubts to speak of, delighted in Chester's serenity. Collaboration soon developed its own routine. Ordinarily in Kirchstetten Wystan worked in his 'cave' and Chester outside, but they used the cocktail table when they worked together. Neither was a bustler nor a brooder, but when collaborating they were like two concerned hens. They delighted in the work. I remember shrieks of laughter and Chester saying, 'You couldn't' and Wystan

'What a pity'. I'm afraid Chester was right. A letter in July 1960 gives an idea of the pace of their work as well as the underlying delight. 'We've been busy,' writes Chester. 'Translating *Mahogonny*. I suppose it is done by now, but we're still making little revisions here and there – Wystan just re-wrote six lines completely about half an hour ago – and Henze arrives in two days with a portfolio full of ideas for revisions, cuts and massacres on HIS libretto, and I've promised to do an article for *Opera News* this month, and I would like to write ONE poem of my own this summer. Oy!' And in 1963 Chester wrote, 'I've gotten a little more poetry done. Not much. But it is difficult to keep one's mind on the line with the libretto floating in the air in front of one. Well libretti are CREATIVE too. And today we must nip into Vienna to see some producer or other who has FLOWN all the way here just to see if he can get the precious and exclusive services of this glamorous team for doing the lyrics of a rather high-brow Broadway musical about Don Quixote. Oh the lovely money if it all works out! Because in any case, the Merrill foundation (which was supposed to have met in May) hasn't seen fit to even tell me whether they rejected my little and fairly modest swipe at their funds. Aren't the rich the END?'

Chester was chronically short of money. When he had a bit he spent it at once, often on gifts for friends. Nothing gave him greater pleasure. I was reminded of a remark Luigino Franchetti made about D. H. Lawrence. Luigino, an Eton and Oxford educated baron, said that the way to get on with Lawrence was always to allow him to stand the drinks. A perceptive observation that could in many respects apply to Chester.

The writing of libretti became more and more important to them both. Wystan used to say it was a pity that Tennyson never tried his hand at libretti, he certainly possessed the necessary lyrical and dramatic gifts, and it might have kept him from writing those unfortunate epics. Wystan loved the libretti for the discipline and the humility they required. An even greater pleasure was working so closely with Chester. Their collaboration went along smoothly until the performance of *Elegy for Young Lovers*, and the severe criticism that followed. Chester, who had done most of the work on the libretto, was troubled by the opera's lack of success. And when a respected critic singled out the libretto as faulty he saw it as a personal offence. Shortly after the Berlin performance of the work, Chester decided not to return to New York for the winter but to go to Athens, alone. They collaborated with Henze again and *The Bassarids* was more favourably received by critics and public alike but, for Chester, the damage was done, especially since Wystan had given an interview saying that *Elegy* was seventy-five per cent Chester's work.

We were all slightly puzzled when Wystan received a letter from a friend in New York who was surprised to learn that they were working on a libretto based on Daphne du Maurier's novel *Rebecca*. Chester solved the puzzle. They were working on a libretto based on Euripides' play *The Bacchae*, which Chester called 'Becky'. By the time the phrase got to New York it had evolved into *Rebecca*.

When 'Becky' turned into *The Bassarids* and had its German première in Berlin, John and I took Lisa with us and went to the opening. Wystan and Chester had arranged rooms at their hotel and were waiting for us there when we arrived the day before the performance. We had dinner in their favourite restaurant. The food was very German, huge, thick plates piled high with slabs of meat, potatoes, over-cooked vegetable, and garnished by poisonous-looking pieces of fruit. The edible parts were delicious. The décor was the primary attraction – the walls were covered with photographs of the British royal family. We found a table in the section devoted to 'Tum-Tum' and Queen Alexandra. Wystan loved stories about British royalty, funny ones, he didn't hold with scurrilous gossip. Once when Chester teased him about a royal's sexual behaviour he replied, 'When royalty does it, it takes place in a mist.' The photos seemed to calm Wystan, who was nervous – he began the conversation by listing all the bad or embarrassing lines he had ever written. Chester was unruffled, almost detached.

We spent most of the day of the performance sightseeing. We went, as most visitors to Berlin in those days did, to see the Wall. Lisa and Chester were distraught. The sight stirred the rest of us to indignation and we passed through Checkpoint Charlie into East Berlin defiantly. The Pergamon Museum was closed so we went to a hotel café and ordered Russian champagne and caviar. East Berlin combined the worst aspects of both cultures; the gracelessness of the West without the efficiency, and the lugubriousness of the East without the ironic humour. The champagne was warm and sticky, and so was the caviar.

The Opera House (Deutsche Oper) was splendid, and completely new to us. The acoustics were well-nigh perfect, the audience enthusiastic and knowledgeable, and the performance brilliant. I was surprised at how much Wystan enjoyed his curtain call, when he made a shyly responsible bow, and the accompanying applause. Afterwards we went to a party given by some friends of Hans Henze. It was in a very modern and expensive house decorated in the latest American fashion – New York, not California. I remember little about the party except that John, seeing Wystan explaining something (in German) to a young man, said to the rest of us 'Wystan is a born pedagogue,' and Chester answered 'Ped-a-*what*?'

When a musical 'event' is truly eventful, everything else seems uninteresting. That is what *The Bassarids* was like in Berlin in 1966. Quite unlike the non-event of the *Parsifal* we saw in Vienna not long after. The excitement of performance was missing, high spirits and enthusiasm were undoubtedly considered inappropriate. The performance took place in semi-darkness behind a scrim. When I complained to Chester he said, 'That's what von Karajan calls staging.' It was listened to with a deadening reverence which the Viennese evidently keep in reserve for this one opera, or for selecting pastry at Demels. Following Chester's lead, I applauded loudly after the second act, the way we do in New York, and we were the only people in the theatre to do so. Cries of outrage and *shsh* went up like pheasants flushed from a covert. A fat-faced blonde in evening dress leaned across two rows and hissed '*Das ist Par-zi-faal.*' Chester, bless him, answered at once, 'Yes, I know. An opera, and this is a theatre. Not a church' – and we applauded more strongly. The man next to Chester said quietly, so carefully that he couldn't be heard by his neighbours, 'You are quite right. This is all nonsense, but what can you do?' Our unsuccessful rebellion gave us a great deal of pleasure, and for years any stuffy or over-earnest type was known as a 'Par-zi-faal'.

Some people say that it was the move to Greece that doomed Chester. Nonsense! At that point in his life any place would have been equally bad. His health, never robust, suffered. The stories he told us – the milder ones to me – were horrendous. I remember a story of his concerning a friend who liked young boys. It seemed that Chester went to his house and saw a very young lad and asked if he was waiting for his friend, who was in the bedroom with the door closed. 'No,' said the lad, 'I'm waiting for my little brother.' Chester was surprised I didn't laugh, which disturbed me even more than the story.

Chester always tried to protect me. He was upset when he thought I was treated badly, and he would say 'it isn't seemly' to so many things where I was concerned. That, too, was hardly realistic, since he must have known that I was far tougher than he was. I had learned how to measure, he never learned. Once in his cups he gave me the most extravagant compliment I have ever received. It was difficult for him to see friends clearly, but with those he loved he always erred on the side of generosity.

I have always been grateful that they were together when Wystan died. Poor Chester died miserably and alone and much, much too young. Chester in all his life was never accountable to anyone. Except for his idolized grandmother, who died when he was still very young, he had no family life to speak of. At school and college in Brooklyn he was so exceptionally intelligent and attractive he created a clique of sycophants around himself – then he met Wystan. He never had to earn his living, nor had he a need for practical contact with his neighbour, and he never had to get on with fellow workers or pupils. Chester was self-indulgent and impossible about meeting deadlines (of any sort), but he was also sensitive, kind and in his own way incredibly generous. And he was forgiving. A letter about a pick-up reads: 'He begs my pardon for the absolutely incessant bad behaviour I'd put up with from him; he calls himself an idiot and a swine (he was but he isn't if you know what I mean); he swears over and over that he loves me; he – Oh why go on. I'm a nervous wreck, my liver feels like a stone.' I learned later that the young man's letter elicited almost every cent Chester had. He never saw the writer again.

Chester scarcely knew his mother, he was only four when she died. Then he became attached to his Aunt Sadie, until she married when he was eight and left his grandmother's house. 'She promised to marry me,' he wailed. He found it difficult to express affection in a straightforward way. His quarrels, like his loves, were excessive. Lovers were either over-praised or ordered about like servants, and not house servants either. He once told me that the only people he was completely himself with were Anne Weiss, John and myself and, later, Sonia Orwell. We had in common the fact that none of us threatened or competed, either artistically or sexually.

When Wystan assumed responsibility for Chester's life, he did it out of love, as Chester accepted it. To Wystan the greatest of virtues were constancy and humility – both were severely tested throughout the years. I have thought about it again and again, and I cannot see how Wystan could have helped in any other way. What he wanted for Chester and himself was impossible to obtain. He must have known this, since the definitions were his own. He, as a devout Christian, was satisfied (too strong a word, but I can't think of another) to let 'Miss God' pardon him. Chester, as a romantic atheist, couldn't. Much has been written about Wystan's love for Chester, but it is difficult for the outsider to recognize how deep the love was on Chester's part. As Chester aged, he became more and more dissatisfied with himself; he refused to believe he could be loved for himself, not just sexually. When he was hunched and fat and balding his gestures were still those of a beautiful youth, and his flirting was outrageous. He could never accept the person he was, so could never become the person he should be. If there had been a point in his life when things could have changed, it had passed. And he knew it. Old photographs show how beautiful Chester was, and Wystan cared for physical beauty. He never thought about his own looks but wanted a certain blond beauty in his lovers. Not like Chester, whose taste ran to beetle brows and sulks. Chester's comic spirit, his wit, his charm were as immediately evident as his beauty; his Jewishness was, for Wystan, an extra bonus.

And then, of course, Chester was not only beauty for Wystan, he was America. After all these years, people still talk about Wystan's move to America and discuss, often heatedly, his motives. I never believed those statements of his about the burden of colonialism and so forth. I figured that they were designed to irritate the English critics, which they certainly did. To me the move was dictated by hope – the hope that America would bring out the best in him – that is, if it didn't break him. He was fully aware of the risk to himself but he was surprised and, if not wounded, at least bruised, by the vehemence of British critics. He was convinced that the isolation would lead to increased productivity; being part of the literary establishment was not only uncomfortable, it was time-consuming.

Wystan's America was, naturally, far different from mine.

He described himself as a New Yorker, and I suppose that description might hold. An American, never! When he first went to America he was surprised to find himself addressed as 'W.H.' by complete strangers. One even asked, 'How is your dear mother?' This irritated him until he came to see that Americans are really quite reticent, perhaps even more reticent than the English. He complained about the 'excessive love of liberty' which he believed to be the basic cause of the anxiety and loneliness he found in the States. He deplored the foreshortening of time in America, the rapidity of change from poverty to wealth, from obscurity to fame, from winner to loser.

For some reason British newspapers, probably in an effort to underline his change in citizenship, began describing his accent as American. Chester and I howled with laughter, but Wystan was not amused. I also laughed at his statement that 'all Americans are lower middle class'. Many Americans did not. Those same people were shocked (as he intended them to be) when he called the sacred Eisenhower 'an old queen with a face like an aged baby'. His views on America became more pronounced as the years went by, until they became as extreme as the climate he deplored. 'Nature never intended man to live here,' he declared. 'Everywhere is either too hot or too cold or, like California, too mild.' He insisted that he never minded being poor in America since the things money could buy were so ugly and vulgar, but had he lived in England he would have wanted a great deal of money. All WASP males were impotent, queer or crazy; the only interesting students were women, Jews or blacks. Wild generalities based on limited but intense observation. There were no trees in Wystan's America, only woods and leaves. He grew to love the States, at least New York, although when he dreamed of 'home', the landscape was British and the food always nursery. The first thing I noticed about Kirchstetten was how similar to the English countryside it was: green rolling hills, hedgerows and well-used lanes. At just the time of the move to New York he formed two of the most important and lasting ties in his life: his return to Christianity and his love for Chester.

Wystan was concerned with the danger to the young of an overbearing teacher, one who created disciples. It was one of his harshest accusations. He felt it destroyed both creative and spiritual growth. He believed a proper teacher, like a proper parent, should insist that a child/pupil become truly independent as soon as possible. Few people understood how strong this feeling was, and I have often heard Wystan himself accused of laying down the law and preaching. I believe that when he repeated himself and made what sounded like *ex cathedra* pronouncements he was merely voicing his thoughts of the moment. As he believed that thoughts should be strong and forceful in order to be at all productive, it followed that they must also be forcefully expressed. Had a listener said that he was prepared to act on Wystan's pronouncements, I think he would have been surprised, and not terribly pleased. He never thought of himself as an apostle; as he said, again and again, his duty was to the language itself, not to the message.

It is true, I think, that Wystan never read reviews of his work, though he cared deeply what people he admired thought of it. A bitchy friend once relayed a criticism that Hannah Arendt had made about an essay of his, and he was upset for weeks. He was, naturally enough, sensitive to criticism about Chester. I often wondered if Chester's extravagances were not in part influenced by the satisfaction he took when Wystan defended him – especially from English critics. As the years passed Chester kept the score of countless slights – real or imaginary – and began lashing out in what must have seemed to him pre-emptive strikes – alas, often at the wrong targets. He began to worry about the impression he made on others. After a visit to us he wrote: 'The enclosed moolah is for Liliana. Do apologize to her for my rather inadequate farewells. I'd felt I should make the gracious gesture of Grazie then, and there I was without a Lira. I felt like a groom afflicted with impotence on his wedding night (I think); a feeling accentuated by the rather limp handshake I gave her.' The letter contained twice the usual tip for Liliana.

He, who seldom wrote letters and never answered by return, fretted if I failed to do so. He once wrote, 'SUCH silence from Flossie Firenze! I ordinarily wouldn't worry but one begins to brood that one has somehow left an offesa behind. Mind you, I'm just an amateur paranoid, but I have my little twitches.'

Wystan's protection was both demanded and rejected by Chester. I complained about the unfairness of Chester's social and emotional demands, but John insisted that Chester saw it as self-preservation, and needed it desperately. One of the few things we never talked about was our feelings for each other. Oh, occasionally a drunken Wystan would say something about *true* friendship or would murmur, 'I know what is right for me,' looking at Chester who would pretend not to notice, but it never went very far, thank God. Other people's love affairs and marriages were dissected but not ours.

They both took genuine pleasure in successful marriages, even those of former lovers, almost as though these made up for them on some celestial scoreboard. They dedicated their translation of *The Magic Flute* to Anne and Irving Weiss because they saw the opera as a 'hymn to heterosexual love'. It was through the Weisses that I had detailed reports of Wystan and Chester in New York. Chester never wrote from there, and Wystan's letters were un-gossipy. In New York Wystan and Chester spent as much time with the Weisses as work schedules and Anne and Irving's growing family would allow. As we did in Kirchstetten, Anne and Irving played games with them, too. A letter of Anne's tells about an evening when 'We made up riddles for them to return riddles that they had made for us. We made them very hard because Wystan is a genius and Chester is frightfully clever. Chester solved half and Wystan couldn't do it at all. So we made him solve them in front of us, helping him out. He grumbled at every riddle – too obscure – incorrect for some dumb reason – and finally I got sore and said "Wystan, one would almost think you would be unable to understand modern poetry." Certain people laughed but others didn't.' Interestingly it was Wystan who repeated this to me in the summer, not Chester. And with only slight changes.

Wonderful letters from Anne kept me informed on important events in New York, like birthday and farewell parties. A pregnant Anne wrote: 'Wystan turned forty-eight with nothing but champagne last Monday and we went. I had to sit all evening which is hell at a crush the size of that party – quite swank and important. Met Ursula Niebuhr who made a beeline for me (what did he tell her?) and we talked babies which didn't interest her but gave me an upper hand so she can go off wondering what the hell I am.' And again: 'Wystan sent himself off magnificently this time – and he won't be back our way for 18 months. He had a group in for champagne and we were joined by the Swedish Ambassador (named Lars or Nils or what) who was terribly elegant, very handsome and very entertaining. At the last minute as we were all leaving, the phone rang and we learned the plane was delayed (it was a night that coincided with planes of all nations slipping off the runways into the bay, but not HIS plane). The Swedish official chauffeur, however, arrived then and sat down to wait until the plane would go and he could drive Wystan to the airport. Wystan said to the ambassador: Well, if I have to wait two more hours, I'll get pickled (then he translated this expression). Outside on the street, the ambassador said: Now, of course, he will lie down for two hours and take a nap. Irving and I laughed and I asked: If you were delayed for two hours, would you take a nap? He said: No, but then I am very nervous. We didn't know quite what to answer to that but I have a feeling Wystan did not lie down for two hours and take a nap.'

When I became pregnant with Simon, Wystan sent me a book with graphic details about the growth and development of the baby. It was sent to me in my third month and he had very carefully marked the relevant passage and pictures.

Wystan alluded to his 'Friday friend', the specialist master-mechanic, and assumed, correctly, that we knew all about him, but the conversation was mostly about schedules. He told us with satisfaction how on alternate Fridays he drove the car to the station in time for the 2.10 train to Vienna, arriving at Hugie's flat at 3.30. Business concluded, they met Hugie's wife at the Bristol at 5.00 for drinks so that Wystan could get the 6.12 back to Kirchstetten and dinner at 7.30. Austrian trains proved reliable and Chester told me Wystan was never late for dinner. I was tempted to giggle, but a warning look from John kept me from it.

Chester, in later years, always had a Greek friend in tow. Whether in Florence or Kirchstetten, he brought one along, usually an Evzone, a member of the royal Greek guards. One of them, named Kosta, carried his own personal icon with him, a tinted photograph of himself in Evzone uniform. It created quite a stir when he passed it around at a rather smart dinner party in Florence. Chester and I swore we saw one elderly gentleman purse his lips for a ritual kiss. The dinner was at the villa of a local contessa, whose husband took me aside and wondered if Wystan would like to recite some of his poetry. Tinted Kosta in uniform came as a relief. Kosta came to stay with us for a couple of weeks in 1965, together with Wystan and Chester, and had himself photographed whenever possible. Looking through some old papers the other day, I came upon Kosta in front of the Duomo, Kosta in front of Palazzo Vecchio, plus a series of the five of us, me seriously pregnant, at Piazzale Michelangelo. Kosta was ambitious. At a formal dinner party at the British Consul's he passed himself off as Wystan's secretary. His conversation consisted of vague Teutonic sounds and when asked his profession he said, 'Ich schreibe für Herr Auden.' Even Kosta must have felt he had gone too far, though, as he assured his listener, 'not his poetry'. When Chester caught Kosta slipping his phone number in Athens into the pocket of the Consul – whose taste ran to pretty girls – there was a scene and Kosta was replaced. 'Kosta of the photographs' gave way to 'Kosta of the tears'. The Evzones have strict physical requirements for their soldiers. Since Chester did his recruiting almost exclusively from their ranks, his friends seemed interchangeable. This, and the lack of fantasy or choice in Greek names, often made things a tad confusing. This particular Kosta had a strong sense of drama, and he and Chester indulged themselves in scenes, accusations and threats that often ended in tears. It was classical drama, and in the original language at that. Wystan and I worried that it might exhaust Chester but John said that we were foolish. John was right and Chester seemed for once to distinguish drama from life: he produced two very good poems that summer. Then 'Kosta of the tears' eloped with a rich American woman and the tears turned serious. A letter that May reads: 'Wystan has told me about all your anxieties with Anita. Isn't it even more awful when one feels in some vague way responsible? You know: was it lurking in our clothes closet waiting for a stranger? Anyway a happy ending. As for me that is the kind of ending I'm hoping for; but my whole life is up in the air right now: waiting for letters, dreading telegrams, keeping myself from making more expensive long-distance calls. And when I am not sobbing on poor Wystan's plump shoulder, I'm conjuring up such visions of profound betrayal as would make the average Othello think himself lucky. There are letters of course: "I'm going away for twenty days to some island with her, but don't imagine I ever intend living with such an evil woman. Don't worry." Ouch. Then a telegram yesterday hinting some dreadful crisis. But nothing definite. The evil one is very wealthy and I introduced them, and she is evil. And so I'm incoherent, and you poor souls are having it taken out on you now. Incidentally, she doesn't exactly dote on me. Certainly the few people in Athens who "received" her, had to give separate receptions to invite me to. Oh well, I'll bore you further when I see you.' That letter was signed 'L'Homme qui rit'.

Strangely, I had met the woman in question years before in California. A trim blonde then nearing middle age, she wore an expensive basic-black dress with a white Peter Pan collar and picked at her food all through dinner. She had the reputation of devouring handsome young men, preferably poor ones (she had inherited money from her famous father). I wrote to Chester immediately. He answered: 'Thanks for the warning, but alas they come in daily, such warnings, and all too late. If only she were a genuine nympho, but fucking is obviously the only "value" she imagines she has. Hence the real dipsomania, the real possessiveness of things and people, the horrifying daily hysterias and demands.' This was followed by a very funny but unprintable limerick describing the lady's requirements. Although the suffering was real Chester couldn't resist being clever about it and writing rude rhymes. I started to mention this to Wystan but felt that the observation would upset him, so for once I kept quiet.

A letter a few days later kept me posted on the Kosta situation: 'I have to prattle in Hamburg the middle of next month at one of those UNESCO things about contemporary musical theatre; and so I may take the opportunity to nip up to Copenhagen. First of all, I adore Copenhagen. And then a selection of the Greek Royal Guard – Evzones – is going to be up there in honor of their Queen. As far as I know Kosta will not be with them, he'll probably still be on his fucking leave on some fucking island – but it will be nice renewing auld acquaintances among his colleagues. After all he's sworn that in our projected future together he'll kill me if I'm untrue. So let's live now. And Austria at the present tempts me like Chow Mein tempts Wystan.'

I wonder what happened to the rest of the first Kosta's photographs, since I can now find only three. I wonder, even more, what happened to the pictures a *Life* magazine photographer took in Kirchstetten three or four years later. The four of us were making The Visit when, by appointment, a pleasant young man came out from Vienna to do an article on the poet at home. We were all photographed around the house. Lisa and Chester making mayonnaise in the kitchen; Wystan taking Simon for a walk; the six of us around the table having lunch, and so on. I was looking forward to having the promised copies, especially one of Wystan hand in hand with a lederhosen-clad Simon. When the article was published it was merely a querulous attack on Wystan's homosexuality. The only pictures reproduced were of Wystan alone, the one with his shopping-bag, and one of Wystan and Chester from which Simon had been artfully airbrushed out. I was furious, Lisa disappointed, John not unduly surprised. Chester was hurt, the journalist had seemed such a nice young man and been given such a good lunch. Wystan was oblivious; he had had a brush with *Life* before. He had been commissioned to write an article on the fall of the Roman Empire. Not realizing (perhaps) that *Life* considered the US to be the direct heir of the Romans, Wystan wrote a piece that said, in substance, that the Empire should have fallen and it was a shame it had taken so long to do so. His editors wanted changes and he refused. He gave them back his considerable advance, which was a severe strain on his finances.

Wystan was not devoid of personal vanity. He was, however, like a beautiful girl who wants to be admired for her brains. He often repeated the praise he had received from Richard Burton. They both read on the same programme in Oxford, and Burton told Wystan that he was by far the better reader. A generous compliment and one that would be contested by many (including me) who had heard them both read. Wystan treasured Burton's praise the way he treasured praise from the young on his agility. Praise for his real work was something else again. I shall never forget his face when a foolish visitor to Kirchstetten told him that a poem of his – it was one of my favourites, 'Prime' – was wonderful, even better than a certain poem by Louis MacNeice. I could see him holding back from hostile comment but the icy tones he used to change the subject told me that in spite of his blue, blue eyes and his natural blond beauty, that undergraduate would never be invited back. When the luckless lad left I teased Wystan about his behaviour. 'Oh, did it show?' he asked. A question that elicited shrieks of laughter from Chester and me. The idea of judging a poem of his in competition was repulsive. The only thing worse would be writing a poem in the hope that it would be better than someone else's.

When Wystan asked friends to destroy his letters I tore up several of the considerable number that I had. Then I stopped, for, truthfully, outside of one very personal one, all his letters to me were filled with practical information or straightforward news. No secrets, no confessions or indiscretions, they were, in fact, rather dull. Chester, on the other hand, wrote long, revealing, honest and enormously amusing letters. All his letters came from Kirchstetten: Greece brought only post-cards; New York, nothing. The letter of Wystan's that gave me the greatest pleasure was one dated June 2nd, the year 1964, although Wystan rarely put that information, at least on his letters to me. He also so consistently misspelled my name, saying it 'should' have a 'c', that it became a family joke. The letter read:

Dearest Teckie:
As I think you know, I am writing a cycle of poems about the various rooms in a house. Here is the one on the Guest Room, and I want your joint permission to dedicate it to you and John.

I saw Anita in London and was delighted and surprised to find her looking fine. She will have to rest, of course, but there seems to be no permanent damage.

I also saw the picture Sheila has painted for you: I hope you like it as much as I do.

Chester seems to have completely got over his hepatitis, and is even able to drink without ill effects.

Am off to the U.S. on Saturday to receive an honorary degree from Swathmore, and return the following Wednesday. Rather exhausting, but since they are paying the fare, I could not refuse to go.

The letter was signed, as always, 'Much love'. Only once did I receive an 'All my love' letter. I include here the first version of 'For Friends Only' that was on the other side of this letter.

### For Friends Only

Ours yet not ours, set apart
As a shrine to friendship
Empty and silent most of the year,
This room awaits from you
What you alone, dear visitor, can give,
A week-end of personal life.

In a house backed by well-kempt woods,
Facing a prosperous sugar-beet country,
Your working hosts engaged to their stint,
You are unlikely to encounter
Lions or romance: were drama your craving
You would not have come.

Books we do have for almost any
Literate mood, notepaper and envelopes
For a writing one (to 'borrow' stamps
Is a mark of ill-breeding):
Between lunch and tea, perhaps a drive;
After dinner, music or gossip.

Should you have troubles (pets will die,
Lovers are always behaving badly)
And confession helps, we will hear it,
Cross-examine and give counsel:
If it hurts to mention the subject,
We shall not be nosey.

Though beginners find it easy, the language
Of friendship is in fact
Very difficult to speak well, a tongue

With no cognate resemblance whatever
To the galimatias of nursery and bedroom,
Court rhyme or rustic prose.

Its idioms, if we use them correctly,
Express as no others could
What matters, a care for the humane,
A concern for one another,
Absent or present, from breakfast meeting until
We part for the night.

In Tum-Tum's reign a tin of biscuits
On the bed-side table provided
For nocturnal hunger. Now weapons have changed,
And the fashion in appetites:
To-day, for the diet-conscious, afraid of thirst,
A bottle of mineral water.

Felicissima notte! May you fall at once
Into a golden dream, assured
That whoever slept in this bed before you
Was also someone we like,
That within the circle of our affection
Also you have no double.

The scheme for this poem is a Chinese one of counted
words, sevens and fives. Wystan had never used this before
and he miscounted the very first line in this early draft.

He had in the past dedicated poems to friends without
asking permission. As to be expected, no one objected but he
found himself in an amusing predicament when he dedicated
'Prologue: The Birth of Architecture' to an architect friend
down on his luck, named John Bayley, and received a fulsome
letter of thanks from the distinguished Oxford don.

It seems strange that both John and I remember so clearly the
discussions, the arguments, the stories and the jokes but

neither of us is very accurate about facts, even important ones. I am thinking of the summer John and I went with Wystan and Chester to a lawyer in Vienna. It must have been either 1966 or 1967, as those were the summers when Lisa was not with us and I distinctly remember that we left Simon at Kirchstetten under Yannis's care. The appointment at the lawyer's was for early afternoon – three, I think. There was a long wrangle about plans. Chester debated the relative merits of lunch at Demels or high tea, and wondered if his shopping should be done before or after. John wanted time to see a show of Egon Schiele drawings. Wystan wanted, in the interest of economy, to combine the trip with a visit to Hugie – but Chester put his foot down on that. All I wanted was to get to Vienna, get it over with, and get back to Simon. Not that I worried about leaving him with Yannis, I had done so before and had returned to find a happy, well-fed baby still pink from his bath. An August afternoon in Vienna held no allure, and the thought of all those quivering delicacies at Demels made me slightly queasy. In the end we compromised. A light lunch at home and then we (John driving) went straight to the lawyer's. I can't remember where his office was. I only know that we parked the car in a square near Baumann's War Ministry building, which I thought impressive, Chester thought grand, and John and Wystan disapproved of as a pompous compromise. We walked about two blocks to the lawyer's office, but I have no idea in which direction. The office was in an undistinguished building built in the early years of the century and recently renovated. We went up in an iron cage of a lift into a series of dark rooms with large windows carefully curtained to keep out any light or air. We were there to witness first Wystan's and then Chester's will. Wystan's left everything to Chester, and Chester's left anything he might inherit from Wystan to John Auden's daughters, Anita and Rita. The whole process took less than an hour, although it seemed interminable. We then rushed to Demels, where Wystan and I had an Austrian idea of a dainty sandwich and some white wine, and Chester and John ordered and consumed an impressive number of *schlag*-filled pastries. We did some speedy shopping and were back only slightly late for the first Martini. There were congratulations all around for efficiency and for remarkably good behaviour, not a single squabble. John and I never thought of the wills again until after Chester's death. Neither document was found among Chester's possessions. I talked to John Auden about it, but as neither my John nor I could remember the lawyer's name or exact address, and the Audens did not want to be embroiled in a sordid situation, nothing was done. The mystery remains.

Beginning in 1964 we had combined The Visit with trips to Prague, which was only a few hours' drive from Kirchstetten. We made plans to take Wystan and Chester with us since Wystan had not been in years and Chester had never seen Prague, but it never worked out. They seldom travelled for the pleasure of travelling; there was nearly always a practical reason. One of the few times they made what could be called a non-essential trip was a long train ride they took to Hammerfest in Norway. Wystan had always wanted to see the most northern inhabited city in the world and Chester rather reluctantly agreed to accompany him. The trip, although they neither of them much liked Hammerfest, was a great success, a success that produced a very good poem. It also gave the two of them some rare time alone without outside pressures and commitments. They brought back stories of amusing adventures and new routines that they had developed; as though they wished to ritualize this experience for further travel. Chester, in deference to Wystan's routine, had brought a thermos full of carefully measured Martinis and disposable paper cups for the long train ride. He had kept the thermos hidden in his case and brought it out as a surprise for Wystan, promptly at six-thirty. The Martinis were poured with great ceremony, and Chester said Wystan had just settled back to enjoy his with an expression 'bordering on ecstasy' when they both noticed that the liquid had eaten straight through the cups. The idea of the two of them busily lapping Martinis from sodden cups cradled in trembling hands still makes me laugh. That the train's conductor chose that moment to enter the carriage to check their tickets is an added joy.

They had enjoyed themselves so much that they decided to drive to Greece in the Volkswagen. The trip itself was a success, in spite of Wystan's lack of skill behind the wheel, the bad roads and the condition of the car. They drove slowly through Yugoslavia, sightseeing in Belgrade, Split and Dubrovnik, and eating prehistoric trout in Ochrid. Their stay in Greece was less satisfactory, as Wystan disliked the *ambiente* in which Chester moved. 'Reminds me of Strindberg,' Wystan said. One of those cryptic remarks that he refused to explain, either because he thought it should be obvious or because he had forgotten what he originally meant. Although he disliked this particular world and feared for its effect he never put pressure on Chester to leave or tried to force him by tightening the purse strings, which must have caused him considerable sacrifice. I wonder if Chester realized this.

In the summer of 1968 we spent two weeks in Czechoslovakia before going to Kirchstetten. Lisa and two young friends of hers were with us, and Simon had been left in Florence. We had all been excited by the atmosphere in Prague, the new opening to the West, the enthusiasm with which we were greeted as representatives of that 'future'. Lisa, the boys and I had gone to the largest cinema in Wenceslas Square to see *Pomoz* or *Help*. There was standing room only and not much of that as the young Czechs discovered and rejoiced in the Beatles. Small groups formed at street corners; sometimes only three or four people, sometimes more, but always intimate gatherings. Even without our Czech friends as interpreters, we found it exhilarating. The excitement was unmistakable and contagious. The boys, Oxford undergraduates, found the real thing more exciting than debates at the

Union, even if less attractive. There was no organization, no order, the orators were scruffy and often smelly, there were no rules and speakers were often interrupted, and listeners wandered away in the midst of what was surely an impassioned plea.

After ten days in Prague we went with Czech friends to a primeval forest in southern Bohemia, staying in a forester's cabin. There we digested our experiences, aided by the cases of Pilsen we had brought with us to supplement the diet of tinned meat (cat food, the young named it) and raw onions that, together with mushrooms and a few berries that we found in the forest, was our diet for four days.

We arrived in Kirchstetten on Monday the 19th August in time for a splendid and much appreciated dinner, and talked until well after midnight. Wystan was fascinated by the street-corner groups. Our excitement must have been catching, as both Wystan and Chester made plans for a trip to Prague. We went off to bed, very late, filled with enthusiasm. The following morning John and I were awakened by a sound at the door as Wystan entered unannounced. The Soviets had invaded Czechoslovakia and he had just heard the news on the morning radio. He sat on the edge of our bed and we all wept.

When the young came in to breakfast and we told them the news, they were indignant and took it as a betrayal. Events had slipped from their control, and they had planned everything so carefully, the way the idealistic young do in preparation for taking over the running of the world. When they were talking among themselves I caught the word 'honour' and thought, 'They really *are* young.'

The boys who were with us that year were interesting, particularly a gifted nineteen-year-old poet, James Fenton. Lisa preferred what Wystan and I considered the wrong one, whose name was Bertie. Chester leaned towards him, too, as he was terribly good-looking and breathlessly enthusiastic. Chester must have been more unhappy than any of us realized or he would not have been so susceptible to Bertie's flattery. John, wisely, kept quiet. I was surprised at Wystan's choice, as Bertie had that naughty choirboy beauty that he so admired. 'Charming,' he said, 'but will not wear well.' 'And the other?' I asked. 'Promising,' said Wystan, 'but he will have trouble loving what he loves.' I could get no more out of him than this abstruse mumble. He was certainly right about the choirboy.

One year in Kirchstetten, fairly early on, we overlapped with the beautiful literary widow. She was actually staying in Vienna, but came out every day for the evening meal. When we arrived, on her third day, the glamour was unravelling. Chester and I volunteered to spend the day in Vienna to help with her shopping, to bring her out for her last dinner and put her on the ten o'clock train back to Vienna. I admit to jealousy – she had that cool, slim beauty and composure that I have always coveted.

The shopping expedition was hell, even for Chester, who liked shopping. He had offered to translate for her, and found the experience helpful from a linguistic point of view. 'Never knew there were so many ways of saying "It's better in America",' he said. When we went back to Kirchstetten and John and Wystan the shopping was still being talked about, at least through the Martinis. We finally got on to a safer topic: travel. That worked fairly well until Wystan brought up their recent trip to Greece by car and the widow said, 'How brave of you! All that way in that little car.' I didn't look at Chester, there was no need.

Digging deep into my memory (as I have been instructed to do) I find the strangest incidents. I remember, for example, arriving at Kirchstetten the summer after 'For Friends Only' was published and Wystan rushing out to buy mineral water for our room. A red-faced Wystan admitted that it was wrong of him to have waited so long to get the vital bottles. On subsequent visits there was never a bottle in the room. Chester and I teased him about the 'truth' in a poem. Chester added that for himself it was only in poetry that he could face truth. It was such an un-Chesterish thing to say that we were all silent. The moment passed without further comment from Chester, and with it passed a possibility. John and I discussed it later with Wystan; we all felt it to be important, but none of us could, even afterwards, think of what should have been said.

Wystan thought that those he really loved were as like him as possible. He once told me he thought of me as his age, though I was twenty years younger. Trying not to show how offended I was, I asked him how old he thought Lisa was (she was about fifteen at the time) and he replied, 'Oh, about the same.' When I described the mirror in my bathroom – so wonderful that whenever I looked into it my twenty-year-old face always smiled back at me – Chester said at once, 'Order me a dozen,' and Wystan said, 'Whatever for?' Wystan was not only fascinated by the ageing process, he welcomed it. He welcomed it as he welcomed all true experiences, gratefully and unrhetorically. As he aged and the lines grew ever deeper on his face, he became almost beautiful. It was as though he wanted to preserve all the suffering and humiliations he had undergone; he was jealous of those lines. Chester, who wanted to freeze his life at its most glorious moment – when he was twenty and beautiful and full of promise – aged prematurely and wretchedly. 'As we were' echoed throughout his work, 'as I was' throughout his conversation.

Wystan and Chester each had a need for rules in their lives. Wystan kept to his 'rules' steadfastly. As Chester's life disintegrated he set 'rules' for himself that were ever more complicated. For some arcane reason he felt it his duty to combat Communism wherever he found it. He was in a rage as he told me of a Greek friend who had voted Communist, in spite of all Chester's warnings. This from someone who called himself a liberal and who cared little for politics. I can't resist adding this ditty Chester once sent me:

Amongst graffiti that I find –
Brags, info, pleas – I hardly mind
Those touching me, the cruder kind,
Flanked by notations more refined.
Boys will be boys: if one's need calls
A spade a Coloured, that's mere balls:
But how I curse the prick that scrawls
His politics upon these walls.

His denunciations of the heterosexual young were equally absurd and embarrassing.

Dear Chester, the great performer whose audiences were shrinking fast. Sadly, as the audiences grew smaller, Chester's performances increased. It seemed to be the one area in which he could re-create himself, the self he longed to be. The attention paid to a star performer was what he craved. No matter that the same stories were told over and over, I often asked for yet one more performance, especially when we were with the young. It was sad that, except for Lisa, who had known him all her life and whose image of him was that of the old Chester, none of the young could see the point of him. One English undergraduate said to me, 'To think Auden could have given up so much for him.' I was incensed and flew to Chester's defence, but found myself saying – to my shame – 'You should have seen him before.' His desire to speak to only one person at a time showed he felt unable to compete for the attention he needed. He would back a listener into a corner, lay a restraining hand on his arm, and talk and talk and talk as though his listener would vanish if he stopped. Wystan never tired of the performances and apart from telling me once that he thought Chester should lose weight, seemed not to notice the change in his appearance. On the other hand, he worried constantly about Chester's health and his habits. We all did. In New York he would leave a party at one o'clock and then go to the San Remo bar. There was nothing any of us could do except pray. It was very depressing, as well as infuriating and disquieting, but it did no good to plead, coax, scold or anything else.

One of Chester's greatest performances was in Greece: the Greece of 'the Colonels'. Chester was arrested by the secret police who had been watching his apartment and been puzzled or shocked or intrigued by the constant movement of young men. Many of these were conscript soldiers who came to Chester's only for a decent meal; many were not. One evening he and four young men were arrested just as they were sitting down to dinner. The four soldiers, who were in civilian clothes, were sent to their barracks and never seen again in Chester's circle. Chester spent the night in the police station being questioned. From Chester's telling of the story it was clear that he put on the peformance of his life. His Greek was excellent, and he had mastered street slang. It was in the midst of his violent anti-Communist phase, and he denounced the evil influence of the Party with such eloquence that he thoroughly convinced his interrogators. After hours of questioning, the chief asked him whether he would come and work for them, and whether he would in that capacity be prepared to kill Papandreou. Chester was so startled, and not a little thrilled, that all he could say was, 'Who? Little me?' This, together with a left hand over his heart and a right hand clutching the side of his face ('Olivia would have been proud,' said Chester), must have penetrated even the thick skulls of the local police. He was released, after breakfast which they all had together, and left issuing invitations for dinner all around.

Not all his adventures in Greece ended so well. He begged John and me to go and stay with him there. Once or twice we had promised to do so, but somehow never made it. At first we said we would not go to a country ruled by the Colonels. After they fell from power we invented some other excuse. We were cowardly, I suppose, and after a while he no longer

114

asked us. Chester's misery was real, although largely self-inflicted. John and I talked about it for hours; we held family conferences with Wystan, in person and by post. A 1971 letter from Wystan reads: 'I entirely agree with your feelings about Chester's mental condition. Incidently, if you know his new Athens address, please send it. Am in despair because all appeals via Alan Ansen have been fruitless, and various people including his future publisher want to get in touch with him.'

It was weeks after this that Chester sent a postcard with his new address; we felt useless and helpless. His shattered health, his dependence on drink and on casual sex (the more degrading the better) were no longer reversible. If it was painful for John and me, and it was, one can only imagine what it was for Wystan. When Chester first went to Greece he tried to re-create the Eden of Ischia. There he had been at the centre, important and admired. The times had changed, he had changed, and he no longer had Wystan with him. All the wishes in the world couldn't change his impossible situation. Though he became unlovely he was never unloved, nor did he indulge in self-pity. He continued to proclaim his membership of an élite, the élite of his fantasy world. Wystan's love remained unchanged no matter how extreme Chester's behaviour, like the love between parent and child.

Unlike Chester, Wystan believed that homosexuality was wrong and that by defying the prohibition against its practice he would, and should, suffer for it. Chester maintained that homosexuality was not only beautiful; it was also right, and that it was Wystan's God and His so-called laws which were wrong. While with Wystan he would behave like a perverse child, starting arguments over nothing, flirting outrageously, spending too much money – in short provoking Wystan, just as a growing child feels a need to provoke his parents in order to make an attempt at establishing for himself his own unique identity. But his provocations were directed at Wystan's beliefs and habits, and never at his work. In all the years and through all the countless hours of talk, I never heard anything I would call negative criticism of each other's work. Certainly I remember discussions about, for example, eliminating the use of the word 'dear' from a poem of Wystan's or '*mi chiamano Mimi*' from one of Chester's. In that particular instance Wystan acceded to Chester's suggestion, while Chester refused to alter a word. These discussions were rather like very serious games, and there was never any rancour. Wystan knowingly let himself (and Chester) in for snide and bitchy remarks by reviewing a volume of Chester's poetry. It was a decision that he later regretted, not for himself, but because he felt it had harmed rather than helped Chester. However, he said that he would do it again as it needed to be done.

Wystan was more open about his life than anyone I have ever known. Not only did he talk about it, he wrote about it. Should one care to examine his writings one could find absolutely everything, including motives, in his life. I don't mean in a confessional way. His confessions he made without intermediaries. He has written more than once about the experience in New York during the war when he felt he must return to Christianity. It seemed to me that he needed something to explain to himself his own great gifts. He was, of course, fully aware of these gifts and was constantly afraid of not using them properly. Lisa once told me how cross he became when, playing cards with the teenagers, he misplayed what promised to be a perfect hand. At first it seemed strange, as he cared nothing for cards and was only playing to please the young, but even in so unimportant a thing as a friendly card game he felt the need to do the best he could with what was given him. He was almost in awe of his own gifts, and certainly accepted the full responsibility such gifts demanded. The thing that worried him most was misuse, 'To ruin a fine tenor voice for effects that bring down the house'. This memorable line mirrored a moment in his life when he had an audience cheering a speech he made in New York raising money for refugees from the Spanish Civil War. Though the cause was just, he felt it immoral to play on the emotions of the crowd with inflammatory words. 'I felt just covered with dirt afterwards,' he said.

He also worried about being proud. Once a very clever friend of ours who was having emotional problems asked Wystan if he should write a book. Wystan answered, 'Do not do anything that will make you feel proud.'

Looking through old letters I find one from Wystan in November 1969 in which he says that Chester had plans to spend his winters in Florence instead of Athens. Wystan says, 'please encourage him'. Chester's visit to us that Christmas did little to encourage me in the encouraging. The accompanying Greek, whose name I have forgotten, seemed not only low-browed but delinquent. This was unusual, as Chester's other friends had a simple politeness and slow gentleness that made them pleasant to have around. This nameless one was different. He was helpful gathering pine cones and Christmas decorations in the woods but he had to be restrained from chopping down far more than was needed. I did not like the way he used his knife. I told John, who promised to keep an eye on him. Instinct warned me that there were changes, unsavoury, even sinister changes taking place. Chester confided that there was no sex; it was just that he had to have someone near him at night so that he could sleep, as pills no longer worked. There was the usual routine of Christmas and New Year's parties, which the Greek seemed to enjoy more than Chester did. I remembered dancing with Chester at festas in Ischia years before. He was extremely good and as I adore dancing we would spend whole evenings showing off. Now he couldn't be coaxed on to the floor and disliked talking to more than one person at a time.

We put all this down to Yannis's recent (1968) death in an accident near Vienna. As we learned the facts the story became worse and worse. Yannis, driving Wystan's car, was rammed by a drunken driver who had no licence. His three passengers, who had only slight injuries, managed to call an ambulance and get him to a hospital in Vienna. There he lay, unable to communicate, as he spoke practically no German, until he died several days later from a broken neck. Chester was in Greece at the time and only found out about it after Yannis's death. Wystan was in New York, and it was from him we heard the news. 'I don't know if Chester wrote to you about our tragedy. On Dec. 12th, while driving my car, Yannis was rammed by a truck (the driver has no licence and was drunk) and was killed.' Chester, at his own expense, had the body flown back to Greece and arranged for the funeral in Livadaki (Arcadia), Yannis's home town. When Chester, accompanied by friends, arrived in Livadaki for the ceremony, he was met, not by a grieving, grateful family, but by the Furies. A group of women relatives dressed in deepest mourning began screaming curses. Curses on the day that Yannis met a foreigner, curses on the foreigner himself, on all foreigners. Chester pretended not to understand Greek and somehow got through the morning. When Chester told us the story, he also told us, in great detail, about the wonderful, simple breakfast he had eaten; to me a very moving addition to the story.

I don't know the truth about the relationship between Chester and Yannis; I only know what it became for Chester. Yannis was a tall, broad-shouldered, quiet lad with a shock of coarse black hair and a nose that would have honoured any Greek vase. When he came to visit he spent most of his time with Simon (whom he called Simonaki), who followed him around and cried when he left. Our conversation must have seemed such gibberish that Simon's baby talk was a relief. Yannis taught Simon a few words of Greek, and they would sit rolling a ball back and forth and playing with Simon's toy cars. After Yannis's death, Chester mythologized him and, I fear, their love. He wrote a moving poem for him, a poem so genuine, the beliefs so truly held, that the facts of the story are unimportant. He had the poem printed privately in English

118

and two different Greek translations. The dedication reads 'For John, Tekky, Lisa and Simonaki, with much grateful love from, I know, both of us.' Yannis was twenty-six when he was killed. Whether Chester was grieving for Yannis or for himself even Wystan didn't know.

### Address

How, darling, this incontinent grief
Must irk you, more
Even than those outraged, mute
Or pleading jealousies, though now
This you are too pitiless to refute,
Making me all you disapprove:
Selfishly sodden, selfless, dirtier, a prodigal
Discredit to our renewed belief in love;
And addressing the dead! You'd laugh.
Yet I can't imagine you deaf
As I know you are and somehow
Hold this one indulgence you allow.
You who allowed me so much in life.

Often during the Tuscan winter we have a spate of fine weather, dazzling, sunny days when it is warm enough to eat outside at midday. We were enjoying such a spell when Chester arrived at the very end of 1970 to celebrate his fiftieth birthday (January 7th). He was in better health and calmer than he had been for quite a while. This year's Evzone, yet another Kosta, was an improvement as well. Kosta was fitness mad and spent most of his time doing sit-ups or push-downs, or outside jogging. He hardly spoke. 'Good morning' and 'good evening', which we all managed in English and in Greek, was our conversational limit. His presence was marked by the grunts that accompanied his exercises and the miasma of the gymnasium that surrounded him.

They had arrived in the midst of preparations for our New

Year's Eve party. Chester inspected the suckling pig ready for roasting in our bread oven, added a few exotic touches to the stuffing, and gave his approval. At the party Chester attached himself to me and then, when it was obvious I had too much to do, to witty, outspoken Sheila Gilmore. I heard Sheila's ringing laugh and knew all was well. Making others laugh was more than social duty, more even than the joy of performance to Chester: it was like bringing to the table a particularly wonderful dish, a giving of himself in the only way he knew how. Sheila accepted his offer with unfeigned delight; Chester relaxed.

When the shops reopened after the holidays we began a feverish search for the ingredients required for Chester's birthday dinner, a dinner he insisted on planning and cooking himself. The boiling, chopping, soaking, broiling, baking were complicated and Chester's demand for preserved goose put a severe strain on our friendship (we compromised with roast jointed duck), but the resulting cassoulet was a masterpiece. Bruno, Bruna and I were willing scullery hands; an excited Simon kept running in and out of the kitchen to watch, and Kosta took to doing his knee-bends in the corner so as not to miss anything. Chester was an excellent organizer; he loved being in charge, and glowed with pleasure when appreciated. And yet, and yet, I couldn't bring myself to take up the none-too-subtle hints he kept dropping. It was clear to me that he wanted to move in and stay with us indefinitely. I failed him as I had failed Wystan about converting the barn. Like Wystan himself, I found it difficult to 'love my neighbour'.

We were going to skip the 1972 Visit, but a letter from Wystan made us feel that was not possible. When we arrived we were met by a shaky Chester and a concerned Wystan. We had seen Chester ill before, but this was different. He had become violently sick in Brussels, where they had gone for a performance of the Nicholas Nabokov opera *Love's Labour's Lost*, for which they had written the libretto. Chester was convinced that the chef at their hotel had tried to poison him, and had become hysterical as well as unable to keep any food down or control his body. He had refused medical help and insisted that daily prayers to Yannis would cure him. There was little one could do. John and/or I sat with him late into the night, after Wystan had gone to bed. He and I talked about novels and old movies and Ischia. John listened to stories about his love life. He was convinced that Yannis had become a saint, and considered himself Yannis's voice on earth. Even the kitchen offered no solace, he actually served us frozen fish fingers. We stayed longer than usual and found him substantially improved at the end of the visit. Letters at the time from Wystan confirm the improvement, which was as welcome as it was temporary.

I never quite realized when the friendship shifted more towards Wystan, because in those first years it was as equal as it is possible. It was Chester who gradually slipped away from us all. I began to notice the superficial change in his appearance first. He put on weight, and his slithery walk turned into a slump and then almost a deformity, partly a result of a congenital weakness of the spine. He kept some of his naturally blond hair and the lovely golden tan, but his Lana Turner looks were gone. This mattered only to him, but to him it mattered enormously; he wailed to me, 'Lana is now my younger sister'. What was almost unbearable for those of us who loved him was the misery which showed with such cruel clarity. To the outsider his face could have been read as debauched, but to us it was anguish. Since he was unable to accept his experiences and absorb them, they became only bad dreams, and as such showed in the droop of his eyes and the looseness of his mouth. One stranger compared his looks in later life to Dorian Grey, another to Baron Charlus: they were both very far off.

Both Wystan and Chester were heavy drinkers – we all were in those days – but Wystan's drinking was, like everything else in his life, on a schedule. Chester started in the morning, and although he was never really drunk, he wasn't sober either, ever.

He tried writing a libretto by himself, it was an excellent one. *The Tuscan Players* reads well on its own, still does; I re-read it recently. The score by Carlo Chavéz was described to me by Charles (I never heard it and as far as I know there are no recordings) as 'wildly Aztec, even in the tender moments'. No one liked the opera much. Blame was variously placed. Some critics even thought they should be able to understand a libretto as it is being sung to them; they hadn't bothered to read it first. Such beautiful poetry and so marvellously singable for the right music, but for Chester yet another failure. And although it happened fairly early this failure pursued him all his life.

He tried Greece. His lovers got worse and worse but his knowledge of the language was extraordinary. He published two more books of accomplished poetry; they were either ignored or compared to Wystan's. He spent more and more time in Greece and drew further and further away from any reality, romanticizing his lovers more and more as they grew lower brows. Wystan never romanticized. One of his lovers complained that Wystan, as a poet, should be more romantic. 'If you want romance,' said Wystan, 'fuck a journalist.'

Chester was touched when we named our son Simon, his middle name, although here again, his attachment to the baby was more imagined than real. Wystan did occasionally complain about Chester, but very seldom. As a matter of fact, bewilderment was what he showed, that and helplessness. I realized, with a bit of a shock, how dependent Wystan was on Chester and not just for household matters. It was the household routine that kept Chester going through those last years. Rather like a juggler who manages to catch all those hoops after you could swear that he had already dropped one, he got dinner on the table every night promptly at seven-thirty.

*

I only saw Wystan in Oxford once, for a weekend before he had moved into his 'cottage'. He was staying at All Souls in lovely rooms that opened on to the Quad and he seemed happy enough when Lisa, then an undergraduate, and I came to fetch him for Saturday tea. At his insistence we went to the café where he appeared daily to meet anyone who wanted a word with him. It was a dreary, formica-topped place that served weak coffee with powdered milk. Not a single undergraduate was in sight, which was pleasant for Lisa and her friend but not so nice for Wystan. He complained that the place was going downhill (in my head I heard Chester's voice saying 'going!') and I was saddened to hear Wystan say that he thought of changing the venue to make it more attractive for any student who wanted to meet him.

The next day I had arranged for a luncheon party at a local restaurant. Lisa and four of her friends were there. Mickey Rose, a great friend of ours, Wystan and myself represented the elders. I knew that Mickey, the son of a bishop as well as an accomplished musician, would be ideal, theology and music being two of Wystan's favourite topics. What I didn't know was how well it would work out with Lisa's friends. I need not have worried; one of the boys, Richard Seaford, was a classicist (another favourite topic), and the others were reading English. It was a jolly occasion, the last fully frivolous time I had with Wystan. As usual when there are decided differences in generations, after the 'shop talk' we turned to family life. Everyone talked, even one painfully shy undergraduate who was so excited he stuttered. Wystan was interested in what everyone had to say. We stayed on talking until the restaurant was empty and the waiters began to fret. Wystan thanked the young for coming. When we walked him back to All Souls, all of us quite tiddly, and he kissed us all goodbye, I felt that the party was really over.

Shortly afterwards a letter from John Auden told me: 'Wystan has moved into his Christ Church Cottage, but finds Oxford noisier and less pleasant than New York. Also unscrupulous people are abstracting money from him and there is a case pending in the courts, against extortion.'

The last Visit to Kirchstetten, in 1973, was spent in a heat wave, one of the worst in living memory. Even the woods offered no relief, they were stifling. Wystan was short of breath but otherwise himself in spite of the disappointment of his return to Oxford. John sat up with Chester every night, listening and trying to help. Chester clung to him, and it seemed that he could scarcely wait for the rest of us to go to bed so that he could have John to himself. I remember the heat, the lack of air and Chester's cooking: for some reason he was into cooking pieces of pork in the midst of the heat wave and we even had fried pig's ear, which would have been bad enough in January. We had to take Simon, aged eight, out for ice cream and a swim in a nearby pool daily, but we cut The Visit short by only one day.

I never saw Wystan again. When Lisa, John Auden and I finally got his body back from the Viennese bureaucrats the coffin was closed.

I wonder if Wystan realized what it cost Chester to argue on behalf of his Austrian boyfriend. When Hugie got into trouble it was Chester who first persuaded Wystan to reconsider his position. Since Chester loathed Hugie it took considerable sacrifice, coupled with a strong sense of justice. Wystan was certainly never romantic about his lovers, but after this at least he tried to see them as more than just paid conveniences. The only time I ever saw Hugie was when, with his wife, Christa, he came to the funeral at Kirchstetten. They were both blond, naturally so. She had a beehive hair-do, long out of fashion, and was dressed in a tailored suit of baby-blue wool that was slightly too tight. He wore the male equivalent of the beehive, sideburns and a modestly priced suit with the short jacket and slim trousers of a race-track tout, although the stripes (black on beige) were as narrow as a banker's suit. Both wore black, well-polished shoes; hers with ankle straps, his with built-up heels. Chester ignored their presence and frowned at Lisa and me when we went over to the corner where they stood to introduce ourselves. He need not have been concerned that we would become too friendly, as we were firmly and decisively snubbed. They stood apart and when Chester, as Wystan had requested, put Siegfried's Funeral March on the gramophone and we all stood in silence, the only other sound was Christa's sobs. I turned my bowed head at an angle to see if the sobs were genuine. They were. Lisa told me afterwards that she had been too embarrassed to look. That must have been the case with the others in the room, too; it certainly wasn't lack of curiosity.

John Auden had rung us in Florence with the news of Wystan's death when I was in the middle of preparing Saturday lunch for some friends. It was to be a picnic, as it was still warm. A hurried search revealed that my passport needed renewing, and a family council decreed that Lisa and I would leave as soon as that was done. John, who had a great deal of work lined up for the following week, would stay at home with Simon. We finally got away at about four in the afternoon and drove through the night, with only a brief stop for a few hours' sleep, arriving at Kirchstetten on Sunday morning at around eleven. We found Chester stunned but coherent. There was no telephone in the house, so messages were brought to the door. Father Lustkandle's successor came to call shortly after our arrival. The leader of the local band came to receive instructions about the funeral; Frau Biba called to take orders for the funeral meats; La D (the housekeeper) was very much in charge.

That first day Chester insisted on cooking, allowing only Lisa in the kitchen with him and leaving me to cope as best I could with telegrams and telephone messages. The accompanying Greek stayed out of the way. I remember very little about that Sunday, and Lisa remembers even less. The next day the three of us, Lisa, Chester and I, drove into Vienna and went directly to a Greek restaurant run by a friend of

Chester's whose Austrian wife had offered to help with the local bureaucracy. She was cordial and willing but ultimately unsuccessful. As the three of us sat in a booth and tried to eat the indigestible nostalgia that passed for Greek food, Chester told us everything he could remember of that last Friday. He went over each moment of the day, often stopping in the middle of a sentence to repeat, from the beginning, the day's events. After Wystan's reading at the Austrian Society of Literature they went to a hotel in Vienna for the night. When Chester knocked on the door of Wystan's hotel room on Saturday morning and there was no answer, he *knew* what had happened and *when*. He was convinced that Wystan had come to him to tell him goodbye shortly before midnight. 'Life without Wystan,' he said, 'unimaginable, unmanageable,' and he wept as though everything he had ever known or remembered or believed about love had come flooding over him. I never saw him weep again.

That evening John Auden arrived, bringing with him a quiet authority that had been missing. Even his presence proved unsuccessful in our struggle with the local bureaucrats. Wystan had died in his sleep and beside his bed were half-empty bottles, one of vodka, one of sleeping pills. To those who knew him, this was routine, to the authorities it smacked of wickedness of some kind or another, and they refused to release the body for burial.

After two long days of unequal struggle I went to the American Consul and within a few hours all was settled so that the funeral could take place. By this time several other old friends had arrived: Alan Ansen from Greece and, to our delight, Sonia Orwell. Stephen Spender was due the next day, as was Wystan's executor, Edward Mendelson, together with Rita Auden and her husband. Anita was expecting a baby within days and couldn't come.

We took all our meals at Frau Biba's inn, and although the menu was limited – I have never willingly eaten goulash soup since – it worked out well enough, except for one rather unpleasant experience. We were at dinner one night when we heard bedraggled music coming from the next room. It was the local band practising for the funeral. Fortunately Lisa's German was adequate and the music was stopped before a drunken Chester or a slightly deaf John became fully aware of it.

So much has been written about the funeral itself, it needs no repeating here. There was even a huge blurry photograph in the Florentine newspaper. '*I Funerali del Poeta*' showed a clump of trees, a part of the coffin lower left and the back of Stephen's head.

After the funeral John Auden wrote: 'I have written to the Dean of Westminster explaining why no cremation. I did not say that Wystan was unhappy in Oxford, but did say that he regarded Hinterholz as his home, and a home from which he wished to be buried.'

Then, a bit later: 'The Christ Church Memorial Service was very well done, and Stephen gave an excellent address. There has been talk about another Service in Westminster Abbey – after Princess Anne has married that horsey chap.' There was also a Requiem in New York at St John's Cathedral. As Anne wrote: 'Billy Meredith read "It's Martini time" very movingly, Richard Wilbur read the Yeats ringingly, Tony read "The Shield of Achilles" very beautifully and Ursula Niebuhr closed with a passage from "For the Time Being" which made me cry. There was a mixed choir which seemed most inappropriate and they didn't sing very well. We have very few photographs and they aren't remarkable. Our memories are rich with anecdotes, most of them funny, but that's about all. The past came rushing back with so many wonderful memories and such a gloomy feeling that it is so much now the past.'

As Wystan pared down his work he pared down his life. In the later years his passion for aphoristic language was more and more apparent. One of his famous tenets was that an artist's life did not affect his work. Perhaps. Certainly with him it was the other way around. Early on he found certain surroundings that were conducive to work. Darkness, cosiness, solitude for short periods, a certain distance and an ironclad schedule; these were not whims, they were necessities. A respect, a reverence for words was all-important. His work was a continual search for the right word, the real word, the authentic word. Chester teased him about this. He sometimes painted himself into a corner, saying, or worse still, writing things he no longer believed. Revising one's work is, I imagine, difficult for many writers; for him it was torture. The continual desire for simplification, the paring down, the elimination of the merely clever and pleasing are all relatively easy to see; what is less evident is the fear and the sacrifice.

The last time I saw Chester was in London. We had both come, he from Athens, I from Florence, for Wystan's memorial service at Westminster Abbey. I went first to John and Sheila's for a drink, where I met the eldest brother, Bernard, for the first and only time. We drank to Wystan. John Auden and I each had a second drink, as we were afraid that the tea party after the ceremony would be just that, tea. Three taxis full of Audens and me arrived at the Abbey to be met by a stately, beautiful Natasha Spender.

Wystan would have loved the ceremony, a full choir and proper eulogies by Poet Laureate and old friend John Betjeman, and Stephen Spender. I scarcely saw Chester as he was sitting with the celebrities, and I with the family. I realized the true purpose of a memorial service; the passing of time had eliminated the shock. How should I mourn, I had wondered? I, who was neither sister, nor lover nor fellow poet? I shall be forever grateful for that service in Westminster Abbey.

The tea party that followed the service was held in the Rectory. It was a slightly stiff and proper occasion. I felt Wystan would have approved the gesture but would have longed to escape.

That evening Stephen and Natasha Spender had arranged a more congenial tribute, a reading of Wystan's poetry by Peggy

Ashcroft and Alec Guinness, to be followed by cheese and wine. How I wept at Alec Guinness's reading of 'Prospero's Farewell to Ariel'. The party that followed was, to me, amazing; a massive dose of London literary life. People had finished their mourning and were now prepared to celebrate, either their place in Wystan's life, or just their survival. Most of the people there had known Wystan far longer than I had. Some friendships went back to the thirties or the twenties, even Chester was almost a newcomer. The Audens left immediately after the reading. As I kissed John goodbye I actually heard a female voice say, 'Who is she?' As the evening wore on curiosity was hidden by good manners, condescension by charm and I enjoyed myself enormously. I couldn't help thinking of the people there in terms of Wystan's poetry. Chatting with Michael Yates I thought of 'Lay your sleeping head'. I met Hedli Anderson and immediately heard 'Stop the clocks, cut off the telephone', and surely would have done the same with William Coldstream, only I couldn't remember *his* poem. Chester was exhausted but clearly enjoying the attentions of erstwhile enemies. I was starving and went off gratefully to a Greek restaurant with 'Installing an American Kitchen', Margaret Gardiner. We didn't mention Wystan once all through dinner.

Shortly after, Sonia, Chester and I met at Sonia's house in Gloucester Road, put away a bottle or two of white wine, and went to a nearby restaurant. Chester had gone to great pains to look well, although the pale green jacket with the pinched-in waist looked sadly out of place in London. His spirits improved with the wine but his speech was slurred and he walked with difficulty. He referred often to Saint Yannis, and it wasn't until nearly the end of the meal, hours later, that he shed the sentimentality and got back to the old, amusing, clever Chester. We hailed a cab for him to go to Fabers. Sonia and I kissed him goodbye. So my last sighting of Chester was of him waving from a London cab and announcing 'Off to Queen Square.'

## Epilogue

Several years later John and I went to Kirchstetten. It was mid-morning when we arrived, driving from Vienna on the newly finished autobahn; a clear warm May day. At the railway station we turned left until we came to the intersection where W. H. Audenstrasse began, then right to the house, arriving at the front gate that had never closed properly. We didn't go into the house at all, as neither of us wanted to face La D and her son, who had taken over the place. The house seemed larger and brighter than it had in memory. The grounds had once consisted of straggly grass, drooping apple trees and Chester's vegetable garden with its snow peas, sweet corn and chervil. Now, all was order and the Austrian idea of a flower garden – a profusion of ill-matching colours. The centrepiece was a discarded tractor tyre planted with dahlias. Wystan, though, would have been pleased to see that the grass was being cut by a hungry goat.

The churchyard was right. Someone had taken care of Wystan, good care. His grave reminded me of one belonging to a British sailor who had died far from home. It looked lost and different, yet superior.